W9-CFM-701

Improve Your Reading

2nd Edition

By
Ron Fry

CAREER PRESS
180 Fifth Avenue
P.O. Box 34
Hawthorne, NJ 07507
1-800-CAREER-1
201-427-0229 (outside U.S.)
FAX: 201-427-2037

IMPROVE YOUR READING (2ND ED.)
ISBN 1-56414-077-6, $6.95
Cover design by A Good Thing, Inc.
Printed in the U.S.A. by Book-mart Press

To order this title by mail, please include price as noted above, $2.50 handling per order, and $1.00 for each book ordered. Send to: Career Press, Inc., 180 Fifth Ave., P.O. Box 34, Hawthorne, NJ 07507.

Or call toll-free 1-800-CAREER-1 (Canada: 201-427-0229) to order using VISA or MasterCard, or for further information on books from Career Press.

Library of Congress Cataloging-in-Publication Data

Fry, Ronald W.
    Improve your reading / by Ron Fry. -- 2nd ed.
        p. cm.
    Includes index.
    ISBN 1-56414-077-6
    1. Reading. 2. Reading comprehension. I. Title.
LB1050. F797   1994
428.4'071--dc20   94-5484
                                                                              CIP

STUDY SMARTER, NOT HARDER!

Ron Fry's **HOW TO STUDY** *Program,* the best-selling and most acclaimed study series of all time, has sold more than 1,000,000 copies in four years. It is used in colleges, high schools and junior highs and by parents and students throughout the world. And Ron has appeared on hundreds of radio and TV shows and countless newspaper and magazine articles and profiles again and again to trumpet his message: Study Smarter, Not Harder!

Here are just a few of the things reviewers have said about *Ron Fry's* **HOW TO STUDY** *Program:*

"These books belong in every secondary library and perhaps in every English classroom. **Highly recommended.**"
— *Library Materials Guide*, Christian Schools International

Table of

CONTENTS

WHY ARE YOU READING THIS BOOK?

All of the now-seven titles in my **HOW TO STUDY** *Program* were originally written, or so I thought at the time, for high school students. But over the years I've discovered that the students buying these books are either already in college (which says wonderful things about the preparation they got in high school), in junior high (which says something much more positive about their motivation and, probably, eventual success) or returning to college (about whom more later).

Many of you reading this are adults. Some of you are returning to school. And some of you are long out of school but have figured out that if you could learn *now* the study skills your teachers never taught you, you'll do better in your careers.

All too many of you are parents with the same lament: "How do I get Johnny (Janie) to do better in school? Why will she spend four hours a day watching TV but I can't get her to read anything more than comic books?"

So I want to briefly take the time to address every one of the audiences for this book and discuss some of the factors particular to each of you:

If you're a high school student

You should be particularly comfortable with both the language and format of the book—its relatively short sentences and paragraphs, occasionally humorous (hopefully) headings and subheadings, a reasonable but certainly not overly challenging vocabulary. I wrote it with you in mind!

If you're a junior high school student

You are trying to improve your reading at *precisely* the right time. Sixth, seventh and eighth grades—before that sometimes cosmic leap to high school—is without a doubt the period in which all study skills, but certainly reading, should be mastered, since doing so will make high school not just easier but a far more positive and successful experience. Although written for high school-level readers, if you're serious enough about studying to be reading this book, I doubt you'll have trouble with the concepts or the language. You're probably just discovering that *The Babysitter's Club* is not what your parents or teachers mean when they refer to "the classics," so it's the perfect time to learn the right way to read and retain what you read.

If you're a "traditional" college student...

...somewhere in the 18 to 25 age range, I would have hoped you had already mastered most if not all of the study skills covered in my **HOW TO STUDY** *Program*, especially reading, the most fundamental of all. Since you haven't, please make learning, using and mastering all of them an absolute priority. Do not pass "Go." Do not go on a date. You may have been able to barely get by with mediocre reading skills in high school, but I guarantee you that college-level reading assignments will knock you for a loop if you haven't mastered all the skills covered in this book.

If you're the parent of a student of any age

You must be convinced of one incontestable fact: It is highly unlikely that your child's school is doing anything to teach him or her how to study. Yes, of course they should. Yes, I know that's what you thought you paid taxes for. Yes, yes, yes. But, but, but—believe me, *they're not doing it.* If they were, hundreds of thousands of high school seniors would be not graduating every year *unable to read.* No, not unable to read and analyze Chaucer—*unable to read enough to follow a map, fill out a job application form or read road signs.*

The lack of study skills training in our nation's schools is woefully obvious, whether the school is in the poorest section of town or the richest, in the inner city or suburban heaven, public or private, elementary, junior high or high school.

What does all this mean? Your involvement in your child's education is absolutely essential to his or her eventual success. Surprisingly enough, the results of every study done in the last two decades about what affects a child's success in school concludes that only one factor *overwhelmingly* affects it, every time: parental involvement. Not the size of the school, the money spent per pupil, the number of language labs, how many of the student body go on to college, how many great teachers there are (or lousy ones). All factors, yes. *But none as significant as the effect you can have.*

9

So please, take the time to read this book (and all of the others in the series, but especially *How to Study)* yourself. Learn what your kids *should* be learning. (And which of the other five subject-specific books in the series your child needs the most.)

And you can help tremendously, *even if you were not a great student yourself, even if you never learned great study skills.* You can learn now together with your child—not only will it help him or her in school, it will help *you* on the job, whatever your job.

Even if you think you need help only in a single area—or two or three—don't use only the specific book in my program that highlights that subject. Read *How to Study* first, *all the way through.* First of all, it will undoubtedly help you increase your mastery of skills you thought you already had. And it will cover those you need help with in a more concise manner. With that background, you will get *more* out of whichever of the other six books you use.

Presuming you need all the help all seven books can give you, what order should you read them in? Aside from reading *How to Study* first—all the way through—I don't think it matters. All of the study skills are interrelated, so practicing one already helps you with the others. If pushed, however, I will admit that I would probably suggest *Improve Your Reading* and *Manage Your Time* be the first two books you study. The former because reading is the basis of every other study skill, the latter because organization is the foundation on which the study pyramid is erected. After that, take your pick!

If you're a nontraditional student

If you're going back to high school, college or graduate school at age 25, 45, 65 or 85—you probably need the help these seven books offer more than anyone! Why? Because the longer you've been out of school, the more likely you don't remember what you've forgotten. And you've forgotten what you're supposed to remember! As much as I emphasize that it's rarely too early to learn good study habits, I must also emphasize that it's never too *late*.

Particular problems of nontraditional students

If you're returning to school and attempting to carry even a partial load of courses while simultaneously holding down a job, raising a family or both, there are some particular problems you face that you probably didn't the first time you were in school:

Time and money pressures. Let's face it, when all you had to worry about was going to school, it simply *had* to be easier than going to school, raising a family and working for a living simultaneously! (And it was!)

Self-imposed fears of inadequacy. You may well convince yourself that you're just "out of practice" with all this school stuff. You don't even remember what color highlighter to use! While some of this fear is valid, most is not. The valid part is that you are returning to an academic atmosphere, one that you may not have even visited for a decade or two. And it *is* different (which I'll discuss more below) than the "work-a-day" world. That's just a matter of adjustment and, trust me, will take a matter of days, if not hours, to dissipate. But I suspect what many of you are really fearing is that you just aren't in that school "mentality" anymore, that you don't "think" the same way. Or, perhaps more pertinently to this book, that the skills you need to succeed in school are rusty.

I think these last fears are groundless. You've been out there thinking and doing for quite a few years, perhaps very successfully, so it's really ridiculous to think school will be so different. It won't be. Relax.

Maybe you're worried because you didn't exactly light up the academic power plant the first time around. Well, neither did Edison or Einstein or a host of other relatively successful people. But then, you've changed rather significantly, haven't you? Held a series of jobs, raised a family, saved money, taken on more and more responsibility? Concentrate on how much *more* qualified you are for school *now* than you were *then!*

Feeling you're "out of your element"—This is a slightly different fear, the fear that you just don't fit in any more. After all, you are *not* 18 again. But then, neither are fully half the college students on campus today. That's right, fully 50-percent of all college students are older than 25. The reality is, you'll probably feel more in your element now than you did the first time around!

You'll see teachers differently—Probably a plus. It's doubtful you'll have the same awe you did the first time around. At worst, you'll consider teachers your equals. At best, you'll consider them younger and not necessarily as successful or experienced as you are.

There are *differences in academic life.* It's slower than the "real" world, and you may well be moving significantly faster than its normal pace. When you were 18, an afternoon without classes meant a game of Frisbee. Now it might mean catching up on a week's worth of errands, cooking (and freezing) a week's worth of dinners and/or writing four reports due last week. Despite your own hectic schedule, do not expect campus life to accelerate in response. You will have to get used to people and systems with far less interest in speed.

Why you're holding a new edition

I first wrote *How to Study* in 1988, convinced that schools were doing a lousy job of teaching kids how to study—synonymous, to me, with teaching them how to *learn*—and that no one was picking up the slack. (I was also convinced—and still am—that most kids wanted *desperately* to learn but would, without some help, find it easier to fail. And failure, once welcomed, is a nasty habit to break.)

Published in 1989, most bookstores wedged one or two copies of *Study* in between the hundreds of phone book-sized test prep volumes.

Tens of thousands of people who obviously needed *How to Study* ferreted out copies wherever they lurked and bought them. In 1990, Career Press sent me around the country to appear on radio and TV, including CNN. And hundreds of newspapers and magazines noticed what we were doing and started writing about *How to Study*. (The fact that test scores had declined for the hundred-fortieth year in a row or so probably had something to do with this, but who am I to quibble with the attention?)

In 1991, *booksellers* started calling to say they hoped I was planning some follow-up books to *Study*. And hundreds of parents and students wrote or called to indicate they needed more help in some specific areas. **Ron Fry's HOW TO STUDY *Program*** was born, featuring a second edition of *Study* and four new books—***Improve Your Reading, Manage***

Your Time, Take Notes and Write Papers—that delved even deeper into critical study skills.

In 1992, I added two more volumes—*"Ace" Any Test* and *Improve Your Memory*, both of which were pretty much written in response to readers' letters.

By the way, in both 1992 and 1993, I added mightily to my Frequent Flyer accounts while talking to people nationwide about studying. I wound up visiting 50 cities, some twice, and appearing on more TV and radio shows than are listed in your daily newspaper.

The result of all this travel was twofold: First, sales of all seven books have skyrocketed, in part because of the chance I've been given to talk about them on so many shows and in so many newspapers and magazines. Second, I got to meet and talk with tens of thousands of students and parents, many of whom confirmed the ongoing need for these books *because very little has changed since I first wrote* **How to Study** *some six years ago*.

Test scores of every kind are lower today than they were then. More and more students are dropping out or, if they *do* manage to graduate high school, are finding they are not equipped to do *any*thing, whether they're hoping to go to college or trying to land a job. And more and more parents are frustrated by their children's inability to learn and their schools' seeming inability to teach.

With so much new feedback, it was time to revise all seven books, all of which are being published in time for "back to school" in 1994. In every book, I've included additional topics and expanded on others. I've changed some examples, simplified some, eliminated some. I've rewritten sentences, paragraphs or entire sections that students seemed to be struggling with. Most importantly, I've tried to reflect my new understanding of just who is reading these books—"traditional" students, their parents *and* nontraditional (i.e. older, perhaps much older) students, many of those self-same parents—and write in such a way to include all three audiences.

A couple of caveats

Before we get on with all the tips and techniques you need to take outstanding notes on any topic from any source, let me make two important points about all seven study books.

First, I believe in gender equality, in writing as well as in life. Unfortunately, I find constructions such as "he and she," "s/he," "womyn" and other such stretches to be painfully awkward. I have therefore attempted to sprinkle pronouns of both genders throughout the text. Some teachers, for example, are "he," some are "she." I think this is preferable to using the masculine pronoun throughout but proclaiming one's feminist leanings or to creating so-called "gender-neutral" words or phrases that I find inhibit the "flow" I try to achieve in my writing.

Second, you will find many pieces of advice, examples, lists and other words, phrases and sections spread throughout two or more of the seven books (this preface being a good example!). Certainly *How to Study*, which is an overview of all the study skills, necessarily contains, though in summarized form, some of each of the other six books. But there are discussions of note-taking in *Write Papers* and *Take Notes*, tips about essay tests in *"Ace" Any Test* and *Write Papers*, time management techniques in *Manage Your Time* and *Improve Your Reading*.

The repetition is unavoidable. While I urge everyone to read all seven books in the series, but especially *How to Study*, they *are* seven individual books. And many people only buy one of them. Consequently, I must include in each the pertinent material *for that topic*, even if that material is then repeated in a second or even a third book. As I will point out again and again throughout all the books, these study skills are intimately inter-related. You can't discuss writing papers without covering taking notes for those papers. Or improving your reading without discussing how to take notes from textbooks.

In many cases, not only is the same topic covered, but it is covered in the same language or uses the same example. If I am particularly happy with the way I covered a subject in one book, I have not gone out of my way to completely rewrite a sentence, paragraph or, for that matter, a whole section just to say it "differently" in another. (Besides, for those who follow my advice and work with all seven books, I think the repetition of some of the same important points can only help them learn it more quickly and easily.)

That said, I can guarantee that the nearly 1,000 pages of my *HOW TO STUDY Program* contain the most wide-ranging, comprehensive and complete system of studying ever published. I have attempted to create a system that is useable, that is useful, that is practical, that is learnable. One that *you* can use— whatever your age, whatever your level of achievement, what-ever your IQ—to start doing better in school *immediately*.

I hope after reading these books you'll agree I've succeeded.

I'm sure after reading these books that *you'll* succeed.

Ron Fry
May, 1994

READING: THE MOTHER OF ALL STUDY SKILLS

I think you'll find this is a book unlike any you've read before. And if you take the time to read it, I promise it will make everything else you have to read—whatever your student status, whatever your job, whatever your age—a lot easier to get through.

Why? Because I'm going to show you how to plow through *all* your reading assignments—whatever the subjects—better and faster...*and* how to remember *more* of what you've read.

This book is *not* a gimmicky speed-reading method. It's not a spelling and grammar guide. Nor is it a lecture on the joys of reading. It's a *practical* guide, geared to *you*—a student who isn't necessarily a poor reader, but who wants to get more from your academic reading—whether texts or the classics—and do better in school.

Personally, I love to read: the classics, spy thrillers, science fiction, sports magazines, the newspaper, the back of the cereal box. When bored, tired, relaxing or eating, I'll read just about anything handy, just to be able to read *some*thing.

But, believe me, just because I loved to read didn't mean it was easy for me to face some of those deadly textbook reading assignments. As a student, you inevitably will be required, as I was, to spend hours poring through ponderous, fact-filled, convoluted reading assignments for subjects that are required but not exactly up there on the "All-Time Favorites" list.

You may love reading for pleasure, but have trouble reading textbook assignments for certain subjects. You may get the reading done, but forget what you've read nearly as quickly as you read it. Or you just may hate the thought of sitting still to read *anything*. What*ever* kind of student you are—and what*ever* your level of reading skill—I've written this book to help you surmount your reading challenge, *whatever it may be*.

You'll learn what you *should* read—and what you don't *have* to. You'll discover how to cut down on the time you spend reading. How to identify the main idea in your reading, as well as the important details. How to remember more of what you read.

I'll show you different ways to read various types of books, from dry science texts to cumbersome classics.

Who knows? I might even convince you reading is fun!

Chapter One

READING SHOULDN'T BE A JOB

Reading is an adventure, when you go with the poets into the realms of fancy and imagination; you see life with the novelist; you go down to the sea in ships and unto the ends of the earth with great explorers; the scientist takes you into the laboratory; in biography you are let into the mystery of men's lives; the historian reconstructs the past and gives you glimpses of the future, and the philosopher gives you a glimpse of his wisdom.
— Holbrook Jackson, *The Joy Of Reading*

You're probably *not* reading this book because you agree with Mr. Jackson that reading is an adventure. At best, reading is something you *do,* not something you *love.* At worst, it is a necessary torture to be endured with the same grim-jawed determination as a root canal.

19

(I don't mean to impugn your study skills, but if you just adored reading, I doubt you'd be reading this book!)

In any case, you must come to realize the vital place reading has in life...and not just in school. We live in what has been called the Information Age—the electronic media bombards our senses with all sorts of sound and picture bytes. But no matter how technologically advanced our society becomes—how large "big-screen" TVs grow, how small CD players shrink, how rapidly the information superhighway is ready to whisk us about—reading is and always will be an essential skill.

And the *better* you read, the more you'll learn and the more you'll be able to become (and the more electronic playthings you'll be able to afford!).

When you're a *good* reader, the world really is your oyster—you qualify for better schools, better jobs, better pay. Poor readers qualify for poor jobs and less fulfilling lives. Non-readers qualify for very little at all, except a life of frustration.

Ready to begin? Get motivated!

Any attempt to improve your reading must begin with motivation. Reading is not a genetic trait that is written in your DNA—there's no gene that makes you a good or bad reader like the ones that decide your hair or eye color. For the most part, reading is an *acquired* skill. A skill *you* can secure, grow and sharpen.

You just have to *want* to. This adventure Mr. Jackson describes is reserved for those who will invest the time and energy necessary to become good readers—for those of you sufficiently motivated to do so.

Within this book, I will address a number of very practical techniques that are sure to increase your reading comprehension. But they are just *techniques*.

You'll invariably find them utterly useless if you are not motivated to read in the first place.

As the Nike commercial lambastes all of us weekend warriors—"Just Do It!" This attitude—not technique—is where the quest for improved reading begins. You must make reading a habit.

Good reader vs. poor reader

Look at the following comparison of a good reader and a poor reader as if you were some corporate hot shot who could hire just one of the individuals:

Good Reader: You read for purpose. You've clearly defined your reason for reading—a question you want answered, facts you must remember, ideas you need to grasp, current events that affect you, or just the pleasure of following a well-written story.

Poor Reader: Yes, you read, but often have no real reason for doing so. You aimlessly struggle through assigned reading, with little effort to grasp the "message."

Good Reader: You read and assimilate thought. You hear and digest the concepts and ideas that are communicated.

Poor Reader: You get lost in the muddle of words, struggling to make sense of what the author is trying to say. You are often bored out of your skull because you force yourself to read every word to "get the message"...which you don't.

Good Reader: You read critically and ask questions to evaluate whether the author's arguments are reasonable or off the wall. You recognize biases and don't just "believe" everything you read.

Improve Your Reading

Poor Reader: You swallow everything you read—hook, line and sinker. You suffer from the delusion that everything in print is true, and are easily swayed from what you formerly believed to be true by any argument that sounds good.

Good Reader: You read a variety of books, magazines, and newspapers—not limiting your reading to the most current "Far Side" humor book. You enjoy all types of reading—fiction, poetry, biography, current events.

Poor Reader: You're a one-track reader—you read the sports pages, comics or Gothic novels. Current events? You catch updates about your world from occasional TV news "sound bites."

Good Reader: You enjoy reading and embrace it as an essential tool in your desire to better yourself.

Poor Reader: You hate to read, deeming it a chore to be endured only when you have to. Reading is "boring."

Take a minute and ask yourself, who would *you* hire? Yes, you might hire Mr. Poor Reader...in some low-paying job. But would you ever put someone with such low-level skills in a responsible position?

At this point, I won't ask you to evaluate your own level of reading skills. Characterizing yourself as a "good" or "poor" reader was not the point of this exercise. What is important is to realize that Ms. Good Reader didn't spring full-blown from Zeus's cranium reading Shakespearean sonnets and quoting Winston Churchill. She learned to read the same way you and I did—with "See Spot run."

In time and through making reading a habit, Ms. Good Reader acquired and honed a skill that will open a world of opportunity to her.

Mr. Poor Reader, at some point, decided that being a good reader was not worth the effort and made *poor* reading his habit.

The good news is that being a poor reader is not a life sentence—you *can* improve your reading. The challenge is to find the motivation!

How fast can you understand?

> When we read too fast or too slowly, we understand nothing.
> — Pascal

Are you worried that you read too slowly? You probably shouldn't be—less-rapid readers are not necessarily less able. What counts is what you comprehend and remember. And like anything else, practice will probably increase your speed levels. If you must have a ranking, take any randomly selected text of 250 words and read it from start to finish, noting the elapsed time on your watch. Then score yourself as follows:

Under 20 seconds	Very Fast
21-30 secs.	Fast
31-45 secs.	Average
46-60 secs.	Slow
61+ secs.	Very Slow

You should only worry—and plan to do something about it—if you fall in the slow or very slow range. Unless you do, you are probably reading as fast as you need to. Again, the relationship between your reading speed and your comprehension is paramount: Read too fast and you may comprehend less; reading slowly does not necessarily mean you're not grasping the material. There are several things you can do to improve these reading mechanics.

To increase your reading speed:

1. Focus your attention and concentration.
2. Eliminate outside distractions.
3. Provide for an uncluttered, comfortable environment.
4. Don't get hung up on single words or sentences, but *do* look up (in the dictionary) key words that you must understand in order to grasp an entire concept.
5. Try to grasp overall concepts rather than attempting to understand every detail.

To increase comprehension:

1. Try to make the act of learning sequential—comprehension is built by adding new knowledge to existing knowledge.
2. Review and rethink at designated points in your reading. Test yourself to see if the importance of the material is getting through.
3. If things don't add up, discard your conclusions. Go back, reread and try to find an alternate conclusion.
4. Summarize what you've read, rephrasing it in your notes, in your own words.

Most importantly, read at the speed that's comfortable for you. Though I *can* read extremely fast, I *choose* to read novels much more slowly so I can appreciate the author's word play. Likewise, any material that I find particularly difficult to grasp slows me right down. I read newspapers, popular magazines and the like very fast, seeking to grasp the information but not worrying about every detail.

Should you take some sort of speed reading course, especially if your current speed level is slow?

Reading for speed has some merit—many people who are slow readers read as little as possible, simply because they find it so tedious and boring. But just reading faster is not the answer to becoming a good reader.

I can't see that such a course could particularly *hurt* you in any way. I can also, however, recommend that you simply keep practicing reading, which will increase your speed naturally.

Habits that *decrease* reading speed/comprehension

1. Reading aloud or moving your lips when you read.
2. Reading mechanically—using your finger to follow words, moving your head as you read.
3. Applying the wrong *kind* of reading to the material.
4. Lacking sufficient vocabulary.

How to remember less...faster

Retention is primarily a product of what you understand. It has little to do with how *fast* you read, how great an outline you can construct or how many fluorescent colors you can mark your textbooks with. Reading a text, grasping the message and remembering it, are the fundamentals that make for high-level retention. Reading at a 1,000-word-per-minute clip does not necessarily mean that you have a clue as to what a text really says.

As you work toward improving your reading, realize that, in the race for retention, speed is secondary to comprehension. If you can read an assignment faster than anyone in class, but couldn't give a one-sentence synopsis of what you read, you lose. But if you really "get the message" of the author—even if it takes you an hour or two longer than some of your friends—your time will pay off in huge dividends in the classroom, and later in life.

That's why this book concentrates only on how you as a student can increase what you retain from your reading assignments. Whether you're reading a convoluted textbook that bores even the professor to tears or a magazine article, newspaper feature, or novel, you follow a certain process in order to absorb what you've read, which consists of:

1. Grasping the main idea
2. Gathering the facts
3. Figuring out the sequence of events
4. Drawing conclusions

When you spend an hour reading an assignment, then can't recall what you've just read, it's usually because a link in this chain has been broken. You've skipped one of these crucial steps in your reading process, leaving your understanding of the material filled with gaps.

To increase your retention rate, you need to master *each level* in this chain of comprehension. Not everything you read will require that you comprehend on all four levels. Following a set of cooking directions, for example, simply requires that you discern the sequence for adding all ingredients. Other reading will demand that you are able to compile facts, identify a thesis and give some critical thought as to its validity.

Ms. Good Reader is not only able to perform at each level of comprehension, but also has developed an instinct: She recognizes that certain things she reads can be read *just* to gather facts or *just* to grasp the main idea. She then is able to read quickly to accomplish this goal and move on to her next assignment—or to that Stephen King novel she's been dying to read.

This book will help you develop a sense of what is involved in *each* step of the reading process.

The first chapters will address these different steps and provide exercises designed to help you master each stage in the process of retaining what you read.

In the final chapters, we will look at how to read literature, how to read a math or science textbook and how to outline so that you can easily review a text.

By the time you finish this short book, you should find that by following the procedures I've suggested, you have significantly improved your reading comprehension.

Chapter Two

READING WITH PURPOSE

Even if you consider yourself "not much of a reader," you read *something* every day: A magazine article, the instructions for hooking up the VCR, telephone messages tacked on the refrigerator, notes from your latest heartthrob.

Regardless of *what* you are reading, you have a purpose that dictates *how* you are going to read it—and you read different items in different ways. You wouldn't read the VCR instructions as you would a novel, any more than you'd read the magazine article in the same way as a grocery list. Without a purpose, you'd find yourself reading aimlessly and very inefficiently.

Unfortunately, many of the students I've talked to haven't realized the importance of having a purpose for reading. Their lack of reading purpose can be summed up by the proverb, "If you aim at nothing, you will hit the bulls-eye every time."

Before you can understand what you're reading—and *remember* it—you must know *why* you're reading it in the first place.

Defining your purpose for reading

What is your purpose in reading? If the best answer you can come up with is, "Because my teacher said so," we need to do a little work to come up with some better reasons. Reading a chapter just so you can say, "I finished my assignment," is relatively futile. You may as well put the book under a pillow and hope to absorb it by osmosis.

Unless you identify some purpose to read, you will find yourself flipping the pages of your textbooks while seldom retaining anything more than the chapter titles.

According to reading experts, there are six fundamental purposes for reading:

1. To grasp a certain message
2. To find important details
3. To answer a specific question
4. To evaluate what you are reading
5. To apply what you are reading
6. To be entertained

Because reading with purpose is the first step toward improved comprehension, let me suggest some simple techniques you can use to identify a purpose for *your* textbook reading.

Look for the clues in every book

There is a group of special sections found in nearly all textbooks and technical materials (in fact, in almost all books except novels) that contain a wealth of information and can help you glean more from your reading. Becoming familiar with this data will enrich your reading experience and often make it easier. Here's what to look for:

The first page after the title page is usually the *table of contents*—a chapter-by-chapter list of the book's contents. Some are surprisingly detailed, listing every major point or topic covered in each chapter.

The first prose section (after the title page, table of contents and, perhaps, acknowledgments page, in which the author thanks other authors and his or her editor, typist, researcher, friends, relatives, teachers, etc., most of which can be ignored by the reader), the *preface* is usually a description of what information you will find in the book. Authors may also use the preface to point out unique aspects of their books.

The *introduction* may be in place of or in addition to the preface and may be written by the author or some "name" the author has recruited to lend additional prestige to his or her work. Most introductions are an even more detailed overview of the book—chapter-by-chapter summaries are often included to give the reader a feel for the material to be covered.

Footnotes may be found throughout the text (a slightly elevated number following a sentence, quote etc., e.g., "jim dandy"[24]) and either explained at the bottom of the page on which they appear or in a special section at the back of the text. Footnotes may be used to cite sources of direct quotes or ideas and/or to further explain a point, add information, etc. outside of the text. You may make it a habit to ferret out sources cited in this way for further reading.

If a text tends to use an alarmingly high number of terms with which you may not be familiar, the considerate author will include a *glossary*—essentially an abridged dictionary that defines all such terms.

The *bibliography*, usually at the end of the book, may include the source material the author used to research the textbook, a list of "recommended reading" or both. It is usually organized alphabetically by subject, making it easy for you to go to your library and find more information on a specific topic.

Appendices containing supplementary data or examples relating to subject matter covered in the text may also appear in the back of the book.

The last thing in a book is usually the *index,* an alphabetical listing that references, by page number, every mention of a particular name, subject, topic, etc. in the text.

Making it a habit to utilize all of these tools in your textbooks can only make your studying easier.

Look for the clues in each chapter

Every textbook offers some clues that will help you define a purpose for reading. Begin with a very quick overview of the assignment, looking for questions that you'd like answered. Consider the following elements of your reading assignment *before* you begin your reading.

Much like the headlines of a newspaper clue you into what the story is about, these elements will give you an insight into what the section or chapter is trying to communicate:

Chapter heads and subheads

Chapter titles and bold-faced subheads announce the detail about the main topic. And, in some textbooks, paragraph headings or bold-face "lead-ins" announce that the author is about to provide finer details.

So start each reading assignment by going through the chapter, beginning to end, *reading* only *the bold-faced heads and subheads.*

For example, suppose you encountered the heading, "The Demise of the American Indian," in your history text. You might use it to form the following questions:

A. *What* caused the demise of the American Indian?

B. *Who* caused the demise of the American Indian?

C. *When* did the demise of the Indian occur?

As you read the chapter, you'll find yourself seeking answers to these questions. You now have a purpose!

Often you may find headings that have words or terms you don't recognize. Seeking to define these terms or explain a concept should then define your purpose.

This process of headline reading takes only a few minutes, but it lays the groundwork for a more intelligent and efficient reading of the chapter. You'll have some idea where the author is headed, which will give you a greater sense of what the most important details are. And clarify where you should be concentrating your studying.

End-of-chapter summaries

If you read a mystery from start to finish, the way the author hopes you will, you're likely to get thrown off the scent by "red herrings" and other common detective novel devices. However, if you read the last page first, knowing the outcome will help you detect how the author constructed the novel and built an open-and-shut case for his or her master sleuth. You'd perceive a wealth of details about the eventually unmasked murderer that might have gone *un*noticed had he been just another of the leading suspects.

Similarly, knowing what the author is driving at in a *textbook* will help you look for the important building blocks for his conclusions while you're reading.

It may not be fun to read a mystery novel this way, but when it comes to textbook reading, it will help you define your purpose for reading. And further, it will transform you into a much more *active* reader, making it less likely you'll doze off while being beaten senseless by the usual ponderous prose.

Pictures, graphs and charts

Most textbooks, particularly those in the sciences, will have charts, graphs, numerical tables, maps and other illustrations. All too many students see these as filler—padding to glance at quickly, and, just as quickly, forget.

If you're giving these charts and graphs short shrift, you're really shortchanging *yourself.* Be sure to observe how they supplement the text, what points they emphasize and make note of these.

Highlighted terms, vocabulary and other facts

In some textbooks, you'll discover that key terms and information are highlighted within the body text. (I don't mean highlighted by a previous student—consider such yellow-markered passages with caution!) To find the definitions of these terms, or to find the application of facts may then be your purpose for reading.

Questions

Some textbook publishers use a format in which key points are emphasized by questions, either within the body of or at the end of the chapter. If you read these questions *before* reading the chapter, you'll have a better idea of what material you need to pay closer attention to.

Prereading your assignment

If you begin your reading assignment by seeking out these heads, subheads and other purpose-finding elements of the chapter, you'll have completed your prereading step. What is prereading? It is simply beginning your assigned reading by reviewing these clues and defining your purpose (or purposes) for reading.

I advise that you *always* preread every assignment! Why? Have you ever spent the better part of an evening plowing through an assignment only to finish with little or no understanding of what you just read? If the answer is "Yes," then you probably failed to preread it.

Purpose defines reading method

Now let's look at how to use purpose to determine your *method* of reading. In most cases, your purpose for reading will dictate how you read.

There are basically three types of reading we all do:

1. *Quick reference reading* focuses on seeking specific information that addresses a particular question or concern we might have;
2. *Critical reading* involves discerning ideas and concepts that require a thorough analysis;
3. *Aesthetic or pleasure reading,* which we do for sheer entertainment or to appreciate an author's style and ability.

As you define your purpose for reading, you will determine which method of reading is necessary to accomplish this purpose. In the following table are some examples of types of reading, why you might read them and the method you should use:

What You're Reading	Purpose	Method
Newspaper advertisements	To locate best price for car	*Quick Reference*
Magazine	To stay aware of current events	*Quick Reference*
Self-help book	To learn to get along better with your family	*Critical*
Biology text	To prepare for an exam	*Critical*
New issue of *Rolling Stone*	To divert your attention from Biology!	*Pleasure*

If you're a good reader or desire to be one: You will always fit your reading *method* to your reading *purpose;* you have trained or are training yourself in a variety of reading skills; you have no problem switching your method to accommodate your purpose; and you are unsatisfied reading only one type of material.

A poor reader, on the other hand, reads everything the same way—doggedly plowing through the Biology assignment and the newspaper and the Stephen King novel...word by painful word. Reading with purpose is both foreign and foreboding to such a person, which makes it difficult for him or her to adapt a method of reading.

Become an active reader

Reading with purpose is as vital to your comprehension and retention as oxygen is to life. Why? It is the cornerstone of *active* reading, reading that involves thinking—that process of engaging your mind and emotions in what the author is trying to communicate. Too many readers seek to absorb information passively as their eyes move across the page. The active reader *involves* him- or herself in receiving a message—a fact, an idea, an opinion—that is readily retained because he or she had a *purpose*.

Following is a passage adapted from another of my books, **Your First Interview**. *Preread* the passage, in order to determine a *purpose* for reading. Be sure to use the note page following to jot down questions that may have been raised through your preread, and the purpose:

Surprisingly enough, interviewers *are* human (for the most part). Like you, they respond positively to those who demonstrate a genuine interest in them. And they become impatient or bored with those who seem too self-absorbed.

Therefore, you can score big points if you demonstrate an interest in the interviewer. This is particularly true if the interview is with the hiring manager. After all, he is looking for an individual whose mission will be to help him, someone who will be attentive and responsive. Showing an interest in the interviewer will go a long way toward convincing him that you will care about *his* needs and goals after you begin working for him.

Out On A Limb

A friend of mine landed a prime position at a brand-new company launched by a legendary entrepreneur in his industry. He was selected over many good candidates for this plum position. This was a triumph for my friend, especially since this entrepreneur, who I'll call Larry, was known to be difficult to impress.

My friend, Cameron, told this story about the interview:

Here was Larry, a multi-millionaire, sitting with a secretary and one other employee in this nearly empty 10,000 square feet of office shell. They had lights, a phone, a postage machine, some furniture, and that's about it. There were workmen off in one corner building some walls for his office.

Naturally, I was expecting a little more, and somehow these strange circumstances completely wiped away my nervousness. When Larry stood up to greet me, I introduced myself, then said, "I bet it has been a long time since you opened your own mail."

At first, I couldn't believe I had done that, but Larry laughed and off we went.

For the next hour, Cameron "had a ball" talking with Larry about the launch of what promised to be an exciting company. He stayed loose during the entire interview, realizing that his going out on a limb had paid off. He felt—and expressed—enthusiasm for the utter lack of structure at the new company and "Larry really picked up on that. I could sense his violent dislike for big structures, so I took pains to stress *my* preference for lean, mean companies."

Cameron's move was risky, but it worked because it displayed confidence, it implied a knowledge of Larry's background, and it suggested that Cameron was well aware that Larry wanted this company to grow to the point that a mailroom would make sense.

Controlling Interest

Cameron had a great deal of control in the interview because he continued to demonstrate an interest in Larry's problems. In fact, to almost any of the challenges Larry discussed, Cameron would ask, "How did that work?" or, "At ABC, we had a similar problem. Let me tell you briefly what worked."

Cameron came across as an interested, sympathetic problem solver. He got an offer for the job that afternoon.

Granted, Cameron was presented with a golden interview opportunity. But he had the experience and *chutzpah* to seize upon it and play it to the hilt.

Oh, Sure You Can!

You're probably saying, "But I can't do anything like that."

Maybe not. It's not often that opportunities like the one Cameron had come along. What's more, you don't have the type of job experience you can draw on to "wow" an interviewer.

But you *can* display your interest in the interviewer with the simplest of comments: "I recognized you from your picture in the employee newsletter. Congratulations on your recent promotion." "Is that a Macintosh SE on your desk? I've heard great things about those machines. How do you like it?" "That's a wonderful photograph on your wall. Where was it taken?"

Don't overdo this. Nothing is worse than "smarminess," unless the interviewer is an egomaniac.

Concentrate, Concentrate, Then Concentrate

Have you ever been in a conversation and realized that while you've been speaking, the person supposedly listening to you was thinking only about what *she'd* say next? You'd probably think that person was pretty self-centered and obviously uninterested in you and what you had to say.

Employers go one step further. They think that people demonstrating such behavior during a job interview are lacking one of the most important skills a good employee needs: the ability to listen, to be attentive, to react to the situation.

During an interview, many candidates have a tendency to let their guard down after a certain amount of time. Oh, they start off enthusiastically and attentively, full of vim and vigor, but once they think they've gotten through the toughest part of the interview, they start to relax .

Don't do it. Don't get *too* relaxed. You should be concentrating on everything the interviewer says and asks so that you can formulate impressive questions and tell him precisely what he wants to know.

I recommend that unless you have an adverse reaction to caffeine, have a cup or two of coffee or tea about thirty minutes before the interview so that your mind is hopping. Just don't overdo it—a fidgety caffeine overdose is hell to deal with during an interview!

Answer The Question

After you give an answer, look your interviewer in the eye and prepare to listen, and I mean *listen*, to the next question. Then give him what he wants.

Improve Your Reading

If he's asked for a specific set of facts, don't lose yourself in a mountain of details and give him all of the implications and explanations he *didn't* ask for.

Terseness and directness will score big points for you. Long-windedness will make the interviewer wish you'd leave and go bend some other manager's ear.

Now, Wait A Second

Many interviewees seem to be under the false assumption that they will score extra points on their interviews if they answer questions quickly. They begin speaking as soon as the interviewer finishes with the question, usually rushing headlong into an answer they soon wish they could revise, or worse yet, withdraw entirely!

It's a much better idea to allow for a short pause after the question so that you can compose a terrific answer.

Short pause not enough? Then stall for more time with phrases like "Now, let me see," "I'm glad you asked that question." Or paraphrase the question and repeat it back to the interviewer. The latter choice would go something like this:

Interviewer: Tell me, what made you decide to change your major six times during your undergraduate days?

Candidate (after a short pause): Why did I change my major so often? Well, let me see, there were several reasons while I was an underclassman, but..." Without a lot of "umms" and "uhhs", the candidate has fairly successfully stalled for time.

(Hey, it worked for Ronald Reagan, didn't it?)

No Question Is A Throwaway

Some questions might seem unimportant, but don't ever *treat* them that way. Give equally careful consideration to every answer.

For instance, one acquaintance of mine thought that enthusiasm and a good work ethic should weigh more heavily in his consideration of candidates for most positions than their experience or education.

So many of the seemingly innocent questions he asked were designed to evaluate to what degree candidates possessed these characteristics. He asked about hobbies, believing that those without interests were either dull or lazy.

He'd also give careful consideration to candidates' comments about the weather, getting to the interview, the hectic days after college.

Candidates who consistently expressed negative views or started whining about these matters were not considered for hire.

So, be on your guard—remember that most employers are looking for enthusiasm, confidence, dependability and vigor.

If you whine your way through questions about the weather, you won't be thought of as someone possessing energy and the right attitude.

And if you point out that it took you hours to find the interviewer's office because you failed to get detailed enough directions, well, so much for your competence and dependability.

Your Notes

What clues can you find that help you define a purpose for reading this passage?

_____

_____

_____

_____

_____

_____

_____

_____

What purpose or purposes did you determine for reading this passage?

_____

_____

_____

_____

_____

_____

What method, based on your purpose, would you use to read this passage?

_____

_____

_____

_____

_____

_____

Chapter Three

FINDING THE MAIN IDEA

In all good writing, there is a controlling thesis or message that connects all the specific details and facts. This concept or idea is usually expressed as a generalization that summarizes the entire text.

Good comprehension results when you are able to grasp this main message, even if you sometimes forget some of the details. When you understand the intent, you have a context in which to evaluate the reasoning, the attitude, and whether the evidence cited really is supportive of the conclusions drawn.

An obsession for facts alone can often obscure the "big picture," giving you an understanding of the trees but no concept of the forest. How many of you have spent hours studying your textbooks for an important exam, collecting dates and names and terms and formulas, but failed to ferret out the main idea, the underlying concept that is composed of these facts?

In longer, more involved readings, there are many messages that are combined to form a chain of thought, which, in turn, may or may not be communicating one thesis or idea.

Your ability to capture this chain of thought determines your level of comprehension—and what you retain.

Dissecting your reading assignment

To succeed in identifying the main idea in any reading assignment, you must learn to use these helpful tools:

1. The topic sentence of a paragraph
2. Summary sentences
3. Supporting sentences
4. Transitional statements

As you learn to dissect your reading assignment, paragraph by paragraph, identifying its many parts and their functions, you'll grasp the main idea much more quickly—and remember it much longer.

Recognizing a topic sentence

Every paragraph has a *topic sentence*—the sentence that summarizes what the paragraph is about. Even if a paragraph does not have such a clearly stated sentence, it can be implied or inferred from what is written.

Generally, the topic sentence is the first or last sentence of a paragraph—the one statement that announces, "Here's what this paragraph is all about!"

When the topic sentence is obscured or hidden, you may need to utilize two simple exercises to uncover it:

1. Pretend you're a headline writer for your local news-paper—write a headline for the paragraph you just read.

2. Write a five-word summary describing what the paragraph is about.

Exercise: Identifying the topic sentence

Write a headline or five-word summary for each of the following paragraphs:

Manicuring and coloring the nails are not a recent beauty secret. Recent archaeology reveals that as early as 3200 B.C., the Chaldeans in Babylonia had gold manicure sets, meaning this practice is at least 5000 years old. Nefertiti and Cleopatra of ancient Egypt painted their fingernails and toenails for much the same reason women today paint theirs—to enhance their physical attractiveness. Historically it seems that cultured, upper-class women through the ages have deemed that coloring their nails is an important part of their effort to be beautiful.

Baseball is an exciting game, especially when seen at the ballpark. Every year millions of fans don their baseball caps and head to the ballpark. Many of these same fans would argue that there is no better hot dog in the world than that consumed at a baseball game. In 1975, fans of the Boston Red Sox consumed 1.5 million hot dogs. With this kind of demand, the traditional method of boiling has been rendered obsolete by technology and the microwave. At Fenway Park and in many other stadiums, an automatic conveyor belt carries hot dogs, already "bunned" and wrapped through three microwave ovens heating them to 150 degrees. They are then sold the traditional way with vendors crying "Hot Dogs!" to all those fans who believe that a hot dog is a vital part of experiencing a day at the ballpark.

As you can see from these two paragraphs, the topic sentence is not always clearly stated. This is especially true in a number of the convoluted textbooks all of us have read. When trying to discern the main idea of such writing, you may need a more indepth analysis.

You can begin your analysis by turning, once again, to our helpful questions. Is the passage written to address one of the questions?

1. *Who?* The paragraph focuses on a particular person or group of people. The topic sentence tells you *who* this is.

2. *When?* The paragraph is primarily concerned with *time*. The topic sentence may even begin with the word "when."

3. *Where?* The paragraph is oriented around a particular place or location. The topic sentence states *where* you are reading about.

4. *Why?* A paragraph that states reasons for some belief or happening usually addresses this question. The topic sentence answers *why* something is true or *why* an event happened.

5. *How?* A paragraph that identifies the way something works or the means by which something is done. The topic sentence explains the *how* of what is described.

You will notice that I didn't include the question "What?" in this list. This is not an oversight! "What" is not included because it addresses such a broad range of possibilities that asking this question will not necessarily lead you to the topic sentence.

The best test to determine whether you have identified the topic sentence is to rephrase this sentence as a question. If the paragraph answers the question that you've framed, you've found the topic sentence.

Summary, support or transitional?

Another technique that will lead you to the topic sentence is to identify what purpose *other* sentences in the paragraph serve, kind of a process of elimination.

Generally, sentences can be characterized as *summary, support* or *transitional.*

Summary sentences state a general idea or concept. As a rule, topic sentences are summary sentences—a concise yet inclusive statement that expresses the general intent of the paragraph. (By definition, the topic sentence is never a support sentence.)

Support sentences are those that provide the specific details and facts that give credibility to the author's points of view. They give examples, explain arguments, offer evidence, or attempt to prove something as true or false. They are not meant to state generally what the author wants to communicate—they are intended to be specific, not conceptual, in nature.

Transitional sentences move the author from one point to another. They may be viewed as a bridge connecting the paragraphs in a text, suggesting the relationship between what you just finished reading and what you are about to read.

Good readers are attuned to the signals such sentences provide—they are buzzers that scream, "This is what you are going to find out next!"

Transitional sentences may also alert you to what you should have just learned. Unlike support sentences, transitional sentences provide invaluable and direct clues to what the topic sentence is.

Some examples of transitional signals

Any sentence that continues a progression of thought or succession of concepts is a transitional sentence. Such a sentence may begin with a word such as "First," "Next," "Finally," or "Then" and indicate the before/after connection between changes, improvements or alterations. Transitional sentences that begin in this way should raise these questions in your mind:

1. Do I know what the previous examples were?
2. What additional example am I about to learn?
3. What was the situation prior to the change?

Other transition statements suggest a change in argument or thought or an exception to a rule. These will generally be introduced by words like "But," "Although," "Though," "Rather," "However" or similar conjunctions that suggest an opposing thought. Such words ought to raise these questions:

1. What is the gist of the argument I just read?
2. What will the argument I am about to read state?
3. To what rule is the author offering an exception?

In your effort to improve your reading, developing the ability to recognize the contrast between general, inclusive words and statements (summary sentences) and specific, detail-oriented sentences (transitional or support sentences) is paramount.

Taking notes

The final step toward grasping and retaining the main idea of any paragraph is taking notes. There are several traditional methods students employ—outlining, highlighting, mapping and drawing a concept tree. (For a complete discussion of note-taking, be sure to read *Take Notes*, another of the seven books in my **HOW TO STUDY** *Program.)*

Whichever method you employ to retain the main idea, focus on the topic sentences, not on the specific details.

If you are a highlighter—you enjoy coloring textbooks with fluorescent markers—you will want to assign one color that you will always use to highlight topic sentences. Avoid what too many students do—highlighting virtually every paragraph. This practice will just extend your review time considerably—you'll find yourself rereading instead of reviewing.

If you utilize outlining or mapping—diagramming what you read rather than spending time worrying about Roman numerals and whether to use lower case letters or upper case letters— you will find that your time will best be spent writing five-word summaries of the topic sentences. If you find yourself getting bogged down in details and specifics, you are wasting valuable time. Again, writers are using these details to communicate their concepts—not necessarily to be remembered.

Read the following passage from an economics text, seeking out the topic sentences. Then summarize the main idea or ideas in five-word phrases.

The Real Economy and Worldwide Capital

Investments by rich Americans do not any longer "trickle down" to the rest of the population. Instead, they flow out into the world at large, seeking the best returns available.

Improve Your Reading

At the same time, foreigners' investments seek good returns in the United States. Investments from overseas had risen to $2 trillion in 1989, an increase of 12 percent from the prior year. Since 1980, the U.S. has seen a fourfold increase in foreign capital investment. Capital moves around the world, paying little or no attention to borders.

Similarly, American money goes abroad as U.S. firms looking for higher profits build factories, buy equipment, and establish laboratories in foreign countries. As a result, although profits earned in the United States by American multinational corporations fell 19 percent in 1989, foreign profits at these same firms increased by 14 percent.

Therefore, wealthy American citizens might enjoy high returns from their foreign investments, but few other Americans enjoy the results. Simply put, the cohesion between American capitalists and the American economy is becoming unglued.

Do your summaries resemble these?

1. Rich Americans invest more abroad
2. No more trickle-down to population
3. Foreign investment in U.S. up
4. American investments down here, up abroad
5. Little connection between wealthy Americans and American economy

Let's try again with this brief excerpt from the article, "A National Care Agenda," by Suzanne Gordon, which appeared in the January 1991 edition of *The Atlantic Monthly*:

> The United States is experiencing an extreme crisis in caring. As a society we cannot seem to muster the political will to care for the most precious things we produce: other human beings.
>
> The United States has slipped to 25th place in the world in its infant-mortality rate. Twenty percent of America's children are destitute. More than 37 million people have no health insurance; 20 million to 30 million more are underinsured. Today, as patients are discharged earlier and earlier from the nation's hospitals, family members are increasingly asked to provide for their complex medical and emotional needs.
>
> It is estimated that 1.8 million women now care for children and elders simultaneously, and 33 percent of women who care for frail elderly relatives do so in addition to holding down jobs.
>
> Yet not only do these caregivers, who relieve our health-care system of a tremendous financial burden, receive little help; they are often penalized for providing such care, through the loss of wages or of the job itself.

The author is throwing around a lot of statistics to impress upon her readers that the United States must give some consideration to people who provide infants and older people with home health care. Should we remember the statistics about infant mortality, inadequate health insurance, the burdens on working women? Should these statistics appear in our notes?

Improve Your Reading

If we read linearly, starting at the beginning and plodding along to the last word, we probably would be tempted to write down these numbers and what they mean in our notes. But, if we were to look ahead in the article (and glance at the sub-heads), we'd find that the author is actually making a case for investments in home care by the federal government and talking about where the money should come from.

Therefore, the statistics are not especially important, but the enormity of the problem to which they give credence *is*.

I didn't always keep my summaries to five words, but I distilled the main ideas to the fewest words I could.

Nor did I always write one summary statement per paragraph, just what was needed to capture the main idea or ideas from each paragraph.

As you review my summary statements, you'll also notice that I didn't include any specific details—no numbers, no dates. Summary statements are only to identify the main ideas. The details will follow.

Chapter Four

GATHERING THE FACTS

Now, what I want is Facts. Teach these boys and girls nothing but Facts. Facts alone are wanted in life. Plant nothing else, and root out everything else. You can only form the minds of reasoning animals upon Facts: nothing else will ever be of any service to them. This is the principle on which I bring up my own children, and this is the principle on which I bring up these children. Stick to Facts, sir!
—Charles Dickens, *Hard Times*

Seeking out the facts, as Dickens's character would have us do, is also an effective way to confront your classroom reading assignments.

While such a "just the facts, ma'am" approach is not the whole formula for scholastic success, you'll find that the vast majority of your assigned reading requires a thorough recall of the facts.

In the previous chapter, we discussed the "forest"—the main idea. In this chapter, we will concentrate on "the trees"— how to read to gather facts, the specific details that support and develop the author's main point.

Facts: Building blocks for ideas

Facts are the building blocks that give credibility to concepts and ideas. Your ability to gather and assimilate these facts will dramatically enhance your success at remembering what the author wanted to communicate.

If, however, you spend so much time studying the trees that you lose sight of the forest, your reading effectiveness will be limited. You must learn to discern what facts are salient to your understanding, and which ones to leave for the next "Trivial Pursuit" update.

If you are trying to identify your purpose for reading this chapter, it's threefold:

1. To develop the skill of *scanning* a text for facts as quickly as possible
2. To distinguish between an important detail and a trivial one
3. To learn how to *skim* text—reading and absorbing its essence, even when you're not looking for anything in particular.

Deciphering the message

The author of any kind of writing should have something to say, a message to communicate.

Unfortunately, such messages are often lost in the glut of verbiage many authors use to "dress up" their basic point. It's your job to rake through the mess and get to the heart of the text.

You need to approach each reading assignment with the mindset of Sherlock Holmes (or Joe Friday, if you prefer): There is a mystery to be solved, and you are the master detective. The goal is to figure out what the text is trying to communicate—regardless of how deeply it is buried in the quagmire of convoluted language.

What is the message?

The first step in any good investigation is to collect all the clues. What are the facts? By spending a few minutes of your time discerning these concrete facts, you will be far better equipped to digest what it is the author is trying to communicate.

But how do you extract the facts when they appear to be hidden in an impenetrable forest of words? You may need a little help—from "who-what-when-where-why-and-how." It seems that the facts readily sally forth when these six trusty questions are called upon the scene.

Exercise: Read the following excerpt, keeping these six words in mind. After you have finished reading it, answer the questions that follow, *without* referring back to the text.

> When told to communicate, most people immediately think of writing or speaking—verbal communication. Yet, there is another form of communication that everyone uses—without realizing it. Through various facial expressions, body movements and gestures, we all have a system of nonverbal communication.
>
> We constantly signal to others our feelings and attitudes unconsciously through actions we

may not even realize we are performing. One type is called barrier signals. Since most people usually feel safer behind a barrier, they often unthinkingly fold their arms or find some other pretext for placing their arms in front of their body when they feel insecure.

Such nonverbal communication can lead to serious misunderstanding if you are not careful. Take the simple symbol you make by forming a circle with your thumb and forefinger. In America it means "OK." In France, however, it signifies a zero, something—or someone— worthless. Imagine the offense a French waiter might take if you signified your satisfaction with your meal with this sign! You would offend and insult when you only intended to praise.

1. One type of unconscious nonverbal communication is:
   A. Barrier signals
   B. Barrow signals
   C. Barrator signals
   D. Barter signals
2. Communicating through body signals is often:
   A. Nonverbal
   B. Conscious
   C. Unconscious
   D. Unnoticeable
3. Through facial expressions and body movements, we communicate:
   A. Attitudes and emotions
   B. Facts and figures

  C. Praise or insults

  D. Friendship

4. People fold their arms when they feel:

  A. Insecure

  B. Disillusioned

  C. Depressed

  D. Ecstatic

5. The thumb-forefinger symbol is an insult to:

  A. The French

  B. Europeans

  C. Americans

  D. Waiters

In the preceding exercise, you should have quickly read through the text and been able to answer all five questions. If it took you more than three minutes to do so, you spent too much time. You were reading *only* to answer our six questions—who?, what?, when?, where?, why? and how? Your purpose was to get to the facts, nothing more.

(The correct answers, by the way, are all "A's"...just what mastery of this book will lead to!)

Scanning, skimming, reading, remembering

Most everyone I know loves to confuse "skim" and "scan." Let me set the record straight. **Skim is to read quickly and superficially. Scan is to read carefully but for a specific item**. So when you *skim* a reading selection, you are reading it in its entirety, though you're only hitting the "highlights."

When you *scan* a selection, you are reading it in detail but only until you find what you're looking for. Scanning is the

57

technique we all employ when using the phone book—unless, of course, you're in the habit of reading every name in the book to find the one you're looking for. When you scan, your eyes do not look at every word, read every sentence or think about every paragraph. Instead, they rapidly move across the page to find just what you are looking for and then read that carefully.

Scanning is the *fastest* reading rate of all—although you are reading in detail, you are *not* seeking to comprehend or remember anything that you see until you find the bit of information you're looking for.

When I was in college, I would begin any assignment by reading the first sentence of every paragraph and trying to answer the questions at the chapter's end. If this did not give me a pretty good idea of the content and important details of that chapter, then—and only then—would I read it more thoroughly.

I'm sure this method of scanning for the facts saved me countless hours of time (and boredom).

Ask first, then look

When scanning for detail, you will often have a particular question, date or fact you need to find. You should approach the text much like the dictionary—knowing the word, you just scan the pages to find its definition. If you must answer a specific question or read about a historic figure, you simply find a source—book, magazine or encyclopedia—and quickly scan the text for the answer or person.

You probably are assigned a lot of reading that can be accomplished by scanning for facts. By establishing the questions you want answered *before* you begin to read, you can quickly browse through the material, extracting only the information you need.

Let's say you're reading a U.S. History text with the goal of identifying the key players in the Watergate Affair. You can breeze through the section that paints a picture of the day's political scene. You can whiz through the description of the Watergate Towers. And you can briefly skim the highlights of other questionable and clandestine political activity in the American past. You *know* what—or who—you're looking for. And there they are—Chuck Colson, John Dean, Mitchell, Liddy. The whole gang. Now you can start to *read*.

By identifying the questions you wanted to answer *(a.k.a.* your purpose) in advance, you would be able to scan the chapter and answer your questions—in a lot less time than it would have taken to painstakingly read every word.

As a general rule, if you are reading textbook material word for word before prereading it, you probably are wasting quite a bit of your study time. Good readers are able to discern what they should read in this manner and what they can afford to skim or scan. When trying to simply gather detail and facts, scanning a text is a simple and very important shortcut.

Alternatively, our ability to skim a chapter—even something you need to read more critically—will enable you to develop a general sense of what the chapter is about and how thoroughly it needs to be read.

Exercise: Answer the following questions by scanning the paragraph that follows.

1. How many days are in an astronomical year?

2. Calendar years have how many days? Hours? Minutes? Seconds?

3. To regain the fraction of a day lost each calendar year, what is done?

Improve Your Reading

Why do we have leap years? They occur to make up the day lost by the fact that our calendar year and the astronomical year do not coincide exactly. An astronomical year has 2,424 days. In calendar years, this is 365 days, five hours, 45 minutes, and twelve seconds. The extra fraction of a day is made up by what we call leap years—when we add an extra day to February. This is done to keep our calendar year in step with the seasons, which are based on the astronomical year.

If this were part of your assigned reading, you would be finished when you had answered the questions. "But I didn't read it," you protest. Can you write a one-sentence summary of the paragraph? If you *can*, and you answered the questions correctly, then you know all you need to.

Skimming, or prereading, is a valuable step even if you aren't seeking specific facts. When skimming for a general overview, there's a very simple procedure to follow:

1. If there is a title or heading, *rephrase it as a question.* This will be your purpose for reading.
2. Examine all the *subheadings, illustrations, and graphics,* as these will help you identify the significant matter within the text.
3. Read thoroughly the *introductory paragraphs,* the summary at the end and any questions at the chapter's end.
4. Read the *first sentence* of every paragraph. As we found in Chapter 3, this is generally where the main idea of a text is found.

5. *Evaluate* what you have gained from this process: Can you answer the questions at the end of the chapter? Could you intelligently participate in a class discussion of the material?
6. *Write* a brief summary that encapsulates what you have learned from your skimming.
7. Based on this evaluation, *decide* whether a more thorough reading is required.

Exercise: Let's see how well you can skim for an overview, rather than for specific facts. Read the following two passages, then follow the seven steps outlined above for each:

Democrats Vs. Republicans: The Real Economy

The cornerstone of Republican economics is that the entire population benefits when the rich are permitted to retain more of their income for themselves. Former President Ronald Reagan believed the benefits enjoyed by wealthy Americans as a result of the 1981 tax cut would "trickle down" to all other citizens. Similarly, President George Bush has advocated lowering the tax on capital gains. This would benefit the wealthy, who own most of the nation's assets, and, he contends, give a boost to the economy that would help the common man, too.

The Democrats, on the other hand, contend that such a distribution of the tax burden is unfair. They think the federal government should increase taxes for wealthy citizens, and that government should spread the wealth directly through a variety of social programs.

Improve Your Reading

The two sides were in a classic standoff through the 1980s. The Republicans were successful in keeping taxes on the wealthy low, while the Democrats did their best to ensure that spending on social programs stayed high. Since members from both camps thought it wise to increase military expenditures during the decade, the federal budget had nowhere to go but up.

In the budget agreement struck between Democrats and Republicans in 1990, both sides gave in a little. Taxes on the rich will increase a bit, and social, or entitlement, programs will grow when the government can pay the bills.

But at the heart of this compromise, which is more like a cease-fire rather than a treaty to end the long war, legislators face the same choices: growth or fairness, private investment or public spending, tax cuts for the wealthy or entitlement programs for the middle class and poor. In this war, the Republicans wave the flag of pure American capitalism, with its ideals of individualism and self-determination. The Democrats, some would argue, represent the kinder, gentler side of human nature.

But is this the real choice facing Americans in the 1990s and beyond?

Many would argue that it is not. And the reason is that both sides are wrong.

The American capitalism so dear to the Republicans is no longer dependent on the private investments of motivated, aggressive American capitalists. Future economic success in the United States depends instead on the country's unique qualities: the skills and insights of the work force and their application to the realities of a global economy.

The Democrats are equally wrong: The role of government is not merely to spread the wealth. It is to build "human capital" and our infrastructure. More than ever, brain power, linked by roads, airports, computers, and cables, is the key factor in determining a nation's standard of living.

South African Bickering Threatens Election Process

The bickering that has gone on among both white and black South African dissidents, primarily over whether to boycott that country's first free elections, is reminiscent of the playground squabbles we went through as children. Bosom buddies one moment, down-in-the-dirt antagonists the next, back in class again minutes later.

Is such bickering merely a method of negotiation, a way for each of the sides, but primarily the African National Congress and the Zulu nationalists, to convince the other that unless their demands are met, they may well scuttle the entire process? Again, is it not like the child who, denied the field at first base, takes his ball and goes home, allowing pride to overcome his desire to play ball, no matter what position he is given?

Perhaps, but the real passions that lie behind such brinkmanship cannot be denied. And neither can the very real sense that for many of the "players," there is far more emotion at work than political maneuvering or logic.

Most of the citizenry is tired of the daily deadlines, the factionalism, the ever-changing alliances, enemies turning into friends overnight, friends waking up enemies. Breakthroughs are announced in newspapers' morning editions only to be proved false by the evening.

This disarray has in many cases overshadowed the active campaigning by Nelson Mandela's African National Congress and President F. W. de Klerk's National Party, the two major factions in the election. Their campaign has been further eroded by the party that has, so far at least, opted out of the elections altogether—the Zulu nationalists' Inkatha Freedom Party. It is unthinkable that they and their mercurial leader, Mangosuthu G. Buthelezi, will hold themselves out of the election process entirely. They simply have too much to lose—patronage, credibility and the ability to incorporate their own platform in the newly formed government—to boycott the elections entirely.

But Buthelezi and his party have defied logic and done the unthinkable before. While many observers believe his holdout to be a shrewd strategic move, one that will enable him to extract every possible concession before he enters the electoral fray, others remember his withdrawal from negotiations last year that many feel would have enabled him to displace de Klerk as the titular opposition leader and expand his influence beyond the predominantly Zulu province of Natal. Instead, he became even more insular and isolated, scared off many former supporters and lost the votes of many who were ready to make him the alternative to Mandela and the ANC.

While it may not be evident at first, you'll soon see how *skimming* can save you a lot of reading time. Even if a more indepth reading is necessary, you will find that by having gone through this process, you will have developed the kind of skeletal framework that will make your further reading faster, easier and more meaningful. And if all you need is "just the facts, ma'am", your ability to *scan* a selection, chapter or book will save you minutes, if not hours, every week.

Whether you're skimming or scanning, you will have equipped yourself with the ability to better digest what it is the author is trying to communicate.

Chapter Five

THE CHALLENGE OF TECHNICAL TEXTS

You've already learned a lot of ways to improve your reading. It's time to examine the unique challenges posed by highly technical texts. Physics, trigonometry, chemistry, calculus—you know, subjects that three-fourths of all students avoid like the plague. Even those students who manage to do well in such subjects wouldn't dare call them "Mickey Mouse" courses.

More than any other kind of reading, these subjects demand a logical, organized approach, a step-by-step reading method.

And they require a detection of the text's *organizational devices*.

Developing the skill to identify the basic sequence of the text will enable you to follow the progression of thought, a progression that is vital to your comprehension and retention.

Why?

In most technical writing, each concept is a like a building block of understanding—if you don't understand a particular section or concept, you won't be able to understand the *next* section, either.

Most technical books are saturated with ideas, terms, formulas and theories. The chapters are dense with information, compressing a great wealth of ideas into a small space. They demand to be read very carefully.

In order to get as much as possible from such reading assignments, you can take advantage of some devices to make sense of the organization. Here are five basic to watch for:

1. Definitions and terms
2. Examples
3. Classifications and listings
4. Use of contrast
5. Cause-effect relationships

As you read any text, but certainly highly specialized ones, identifying these devices will help you grasp the main idea, as well as any details that are essential to your thorough understanding of the material.

Definitions and terminology

In reading any specialized text, you must begin at the beginning—understanding the terms particular to that discipline. Familiar, everyday words have very precise definitions in technical writing.

What do I mean? Take the word *nice*. You may compliment your friend's new sweater, telling her it's *nice,* meaning attractive. You may find that the new chemistry teacher is *nice,* meaning he doesn't give too much homework. And when your friend uses the word *nice* to describe the blind date she's set up for you, it may mean something completely different—and insidious.

Everyday words can have a variety of meanings, some of them even contradictory, depending on the context in which they're used.

In contrast, in the sciences, terminology has fixed and specific meanings. For example, the definition of elasticity—*"the ability of a solid to regain its shape after a deforming force has been applied"*—is the same in Bangkok or Brooklyn. Such exact terminology enables scientists to communicate with the kind of precision their discipline requires.

Definitions may vary in length. One term may require a one-sentence definition, others merit entire paragraphs. Some may even need a whole chapter to accurately communicate the definition.

Examples help clarify the abstract

A second communication tool is the example. Authors use such examples to bridge abstract principles to concrete illustrations. These examples are essential to your ability to comprehend intricate and complicated theories.

Unlike other writing, technical writing places a very high premium on brevity. Economizing words is the key to covering a large volume of knowledge in a relatively short space. Few technical texts or articles include anecdotal matter or chatty stories of the author's experience.

This fact challenges the reader to pay particular attention to the examples that are included. Why? Technical writing often is filled with new or foreign ideas—many of which are not readily digestible. They are difficult in part because they are abstract. Examples work to clarify these concepts, hopefully in terms more easily understood.

For example, it may be difficult for you to make sense of the definition for symbiosis—*"the living together of two dissimilar organisms, especially when mutually beneficial"*—but the example of the bird that picks food from the crocodile's teeth, thereby feeding itself and keeping the crocodile cavity-free, helps bring it home.

Classification and listings

A third tool frequently utilized in texts is classification and listings. Classifying is the process by which subjects that are common are categorized under a general heading.

Some examples:

Matter may occur in three forms: solid, liquid or gas.
    Classification: Three forms of matter
    Listing: Solid, liquid, gas

The social sciences are psychology, economics, and sociology.
    Classification: Social sciences
    Listing: Psychology, economics, sociology

Especially in technical writing, authors use classification to categorize extensive lists of detail. Such writings may have several categories and subcategories that organize these details into some manageable fashion.

Comparing/Contrasting

A fourth tool used in communicating difficult information is that of comparing and contrasting. Texts use this tool to bring complicated material into focus by offering an opposing picture or one that is similar.

Such devices are invaluable in grasping concepts that do not conjure a picture in your mind. Gravity, for example, is not something that can be readily pictured—it's not a tangible, touchable object that can be described.

Through comparison, a text relates a concept to one that has been previously defined—or to one a reader may readily understand. Through contrast, the text concentrates on the differences and distinctions between two ideas. By focusing on distinguishing features, these ideas become clearer as one idea is held up against another.

Cause-effect relationships

A final tool that texts employ to communicate is that of cause-effect relationships. This device is best defined in the context of science ,where it is the fundamental quest of most scientific research.

Science begins with the observation of the effect—what is happening?

It is snowing.

The next step is to conduct research into the cause: *Why* is it snowing? Detailing this cause-effect relationship is often the essence of scientific and technical writing.

Cause-effect relationships may be written in many ways. The effect may be stated first, followed by the cause. An effect may be the result of several connected causes—a causal chain. And a cause may have numerous effects.

In your reading, it is vital that you recognize this relationship and its significance.

Read with a plan

More than any other type of writing, highly specialized, technical writing must be read with a plan. You can't approach your reading assignment merely with the goal of completing it. Such mindless reading will leave you confused and frustrated, drowning in a quagmire of theory, concepts, terms and examples.

Your plan should incorporate the following guidelines:

1. *Learn the terms* that are essential to understanding the concepts presented. Knowing the precise definitions that the author uses will enable you to follow his chain of thought through the text.

2. *Determine the structure or organization of the text.* Most chapters have a definite pattern that forms the skeleton of the material. A book may begin with a statement of a theory, give examples, provide sample problems, then summarize. Often this pattern can be discerned through a preview of the table of contents or the titles and subtitles.

3. *Skim the chapter* to get a sense of the author's viewpoint. Ask questions to define your purpose in reading. Use any summaries or review questions to guide your reading.

4. Do a *thorough, analytical reading* of the text. Do not proceed from one section to the next until you have a clear understanding of the section you are reading. The concepts generally build upon each other. To proceed to a new section without understanding the ones that precede it is, at best, futile.

5. Immediately upon concluding your thorough reading, *review!* Write a summary of the concepts and theories you need to remember. Answer any questions raised when you skimmed of the text. Do the problems. If possible, apply the formulas.

Improve Your Reading

Technical material is saturated with ideas. When reading it, you must be convinced of one fact: Every word counts! You will want to read such material with the utmost concentration—it is not meant to be sped through.

Good readers know that such material demands a slow read that concentrates on achieving the greatest level of retention.

Every definition has to be digested.

Every formula committed to memory.

Every example considered.

To improve your reading of such technical material you will want to hone the skill of identifying the devices an author uses to communicate. In so doing, you will be able to connect the chain of thought that occurs. When reading such texts—or attempting to work out technical problems—try the following "tricks":

- Whenever you can, "translate" formulas and numbers into words. To test your understanding, try to put your translation into *different* words.

- Even if you're not particularly visual, pictures can often help. Try translating a particularly vexing math problem into a drawing or diagram.

- Before you even get down to solving a problem, is there any way for you to estimate the answer or, at least, to estimate the range within which the answer should fall (greater than 1, but less than 10)? This is the easy way to at least make sure you wind up in the right ballpark.

- Play around. There are often different paths to the same solution, or even equally valid solutions. If you find one, try to find others. This a great way to increase your understanding of all the principles involved.

- When you are checking your calculations, try working *back*wards. I've found it an easier way to catch simple arithmetical errors.

- Try to figure out what is being asked, what principles are involved, what information is important, what's not. (I can't resist an example here, one that was thrown at me in 8th grade: Picture a record—the vinyl kind, before CDs. Its diameter is 9 inches. The label is perfectly centered. Its radius is 1.75 inches. The record plays at 45 revolutions per minute, and the song it plays lasts for exactly 3 minutes. The vinyl is exactly .18 mm thick.

  Got it? OK, here's the question: How many grooves does the record have?)

- Teach someone else. Trying to explain mathematical concepts to someone else will quickly pinpoint what you really know or don't know. It's virtually impossible to get someone else—especially someone who is slower than you at all this stuff—to understand if you don't!

  (By the way, the answer is "one." Any *more* than one continuous groove and the song wouldn't keep playing. In case you didn't notice, *none* of the mathematical information given had the slightest bearing on the answer.)

Chapter Six

BECOMING A CRITICAL READER

Analyze and interpret the following statements:

How The Art Of Reasoning Is Necessary

When one of his audience said, "Convince me that logic is useful," he said, "Would you have me demonstrate it?"

"Yes."

"Well, then, must I not use a demonstrative argument?"

And, when the other agreed, he said, "How then shall you know if I impose upon you?"

And when the man had no answer, he said, "You see how you yourself admit that logic is necessary, if without it you are not even able to learn this much—whether it is necessary or not."

"In a republican nation, whose citizens are to be led by reason and persuasion and not by force, the art of reasoning becomes of first importance."
— Thomas Jefferson

"Anyway, I keep picturing all these little kids playing some game in this big field of rye and all. Thousands of little kids, and nobody's around— nobody big, I mean, except me. And I'm standing on the edge of some crazy cliff. What I have to do, I have to catch everybody if they start to go over the cliff—I mean if they're running and they don't look where they're going I have to come out from somewhere and catch them. That's all I'd do all day. I'd just be the catcher in the rye..."
— Excerpt from J.D. Salinger, *Catcher In The Rye*

"He who has a why to live can bear with almost any how."
— Nietzsche

After four years of undergraduate work, before my dear alma mater would award me the degree for which I felt my dollars, sweat and blood had amply paid, I was made to endure a six-hour essay test that began much like your instructions here. We literature majors were given one question—"Analyze and interpret the following:" The "following" being a poem we had never seen before...and several blue books in which to write our erudite answers.

Unbelievable?

Hardly!

This test was given in much the same way that the Educational Testing Service gives their PSAT, SAT, LSAT and GMAT verbal tests. In the notorious reading comprehension section, you are required to read a distilled passage—which, unless you've stolen a peek at the exam, you have never seen— and then given four to six questions to determine if you have any clue as to what you just read.

You will find that there are many times, particularly in comparative literature classes, when you will need to read something with great care in order to remember details and interpret meaning. Hester Prynne's red monogram, Poe's talking raven and Ponzo's and Lucky's mysterious friend all require a little more analysis than a superficial interpretation of props and plot.

Yet such detailed, analytical reading is not limited to literature. Political dissertations, historical analysis and even scientific research may each require more careful reading than the latest "space opera."

Such reading is often referred to as *critical reading,* a type of reading during which you seek to distinguish thoughts, ideas or concepts—each demanding thorough study and evaluation.

Critical reading requires that you are able to identify the author's arguments, measure their worth and truth and apply what is pertinent to your own experience. Unlike skimming, critical reading challenges the reader to concentrate at the highest level possible.

Prepare yourself to read critically

When preparing to read critically, you must lay the groundwork for concentration. Just as an athlete must ready himself mentally to achieve peak performance, you will want to ready yourself before you begin to read.

The following suggestions will help you prepare to read critically:

1. You must have a clearly defined purpose for reading. Make sure that you've identified your purpose before you begin.

2. Pay attention! Avoid letting your mind wander to that conversation you and your friend had today at lunch. Minimize distractions and interruptions—anything or anyone that causes you to break your focus.

3. Find your optimum study environment—a quiet corner in the library, your own room, wherever. In absolute silence, or with your new CD playing. (Be sure to read *Manage Your Time*, another of the seven books in my **HOW TO STUDY** *Program*, for more tips on finding *your* perfect study environment.)

4. Don't worry about how fast or slowly you read. Your goal should be to understand the material, not to find out "How fast can I get this over with?"

5. If it seems that you will need several hours to complete your reading, you might break the longer assignments into smaller, more manageable, parts, then reward yourself at the end of each of these sections by taking brief breaks.

If you take these steps prior to reading any text that requires your utmost concentration, you will find that your mind is readied for the kind of focus necessary to read critically. Make a *habit* of such preparations, and you will set yourself up to succeed.

Prereading is a must

Once you have prepared your mind to read, the next step is to understand the "big picture"—what is the author's thesis or main idea? Good comprehension is the consequence of your ability to grasp the main point of what the author is trying to communicate.

Grasping this message is accomplished through skimming, as we discussed in Chapter 4. Let's review the basic steps:

1. If there is a title or heading, rephrase it as a question. This will support your purpose for reading.

2. Examine all the subheadings, illustrations and graphics, as these will help you identify the significant matter within the text.

3. Read the introductory paragraphs, the summary and any questions at the end of the chapter.

4. Read the first sentence of every paragraph. In Chapter 3, you learned that this is generally where the main idea is found.

5. Evaluate what you have gained from this process: Can you answer the question's at the chapter's end? Could you intelligently participate in a class discussion of the material?

6. Write a brief summary of what you have learned from your skimming.

By beginning your critical reading with a 20-minute "skim" of the text, you should be ready to answer three questions:

1. What is the text's principal message or viewpoint?

2. Is an obvious chain of thought or reasoning revealed?

3. What major points are addressed?

Now, *read* it

Once you identify and understand the basic skeleton of the material, your actual "read" of the material—following the details, reasoning, and chain of thought—is simply a matter of attaching meat to the bones.

This digestive process involves learning to interpret and evaluate what is written, what is directly stated and what can be inferred from the context.

Effective analytical reading requires that you, the reader, distinguish the explicit, literal meaning of words *(denotation)* and what suggestions or intentions are intimated by the general content *(connotation)*.

Analyzing: What the words *connote*

Words and writing have two levels of meaning that are important to the reader's comprehension.

The first level is the literal or descriptive meaning. What a word expressly *denotes*—the specific, precise definition you'd find in *Webster*.

Connotation involves this second level of meaning—that which incorporates the total *significance* of the words.

What does that mean?

Beyond a literal definition, words communicate emotion, bias, attitude, and perspective. Analyzing any text involves learning to interpret what is implied, just as much as what is expressly stated.

Improve Your Reading

The following brainteasers challenge you to read beyond what is expressly stated.

Bill is being imprisoned by terrorists in a building that has triple locks on the door. The walls are steel-reinforced concrete and the floor is packed earth. In the middle of the ceiling, well above Bill's head is an air vent just wide enough for a man to squeeze through. There is nothing in the room for Bill to stand on to reach the vent. One night well after dark Bill escapes. How?

Matt and Candie are having a very serious game of golf—the loser buys dinner. Late in the game, with the score very close, Matt's ball rolls inside a paper bag that has been left on the course. Rules prohibit Matt from touching the bag or removing the ball from the bag. Candie insists that he not break the rule. What can Matt do to get a clear shot on his ball?

Personally, I hate brainteasers, but they are nothing compared to some of the books I was required to read in school. Textbooks, literature, and many of your reading assignments will be just as convoluted as these questions (even though their authors have not, we are assured, gone out of their way to make their books so obtuse on purpose). You will greatly increase your comprehension as you read for implicit meaning and for inference.

(Oh, you want the answers to the brainteasers? In the first one, Bill escaped from his cell by digging a hole in the packed-earth floor and climbing on top of the pile of earth to reach the vent. In the second brainteaser, Matt simply lit a match and burned the bag around his golf ball. Did you guess them?)

15 questions to help you

Beyond grasping the meaning of words and phrases, critical reading requires that you ask questions. Here are 15 questions that will help you effectively analyze and interpret most of what you read.

1. Is there a clear message communicated throughout?
2. Are the relationships between the points direct and clear?
3. Is there a relationship between your experience and the author's?
4. Are the details factual?
5. Are the examples and evidence relevant?
6. Is there consistency of thought?
7. What is the author's bias or slant?
8. What is the author's motive?
9. What does the author want you to believe?
10. Does this jibe with your own belief or experience?
11. Is the author rational or subjective?
12. Is there a confusion between feelings and facts?
13. Are the main points logically ordered?
14. Are the arguments and conclusions consistent?
15. Are the explanations clear?

Obviously, this list of questions is not all inclusive. But, it will give you a jumpstart when critical reading is required. Remember, the essential ingredient to any effective analysis and interpretation is the questions you ask.

Summarizing: The final step

The final step in any critical reading is that of summarizing. Nothing will be more important to your recall than learning to condense what you read into a clear and concise summary.

Many of you have learned to do this by excerpting entire segments or sentences from a text, certainly not a very efficient method for summarizing.

I recommend using the traditional outline (which is explained in detail in my book, *Take Notes*, yet another in my **HOW TO STUDY** *Program*)

Another suggestion is to use a two-step process called *diagramming,* which calls for the reader to *diagram* or illustrate that content that he's just read, then to write a brief synopsis of what he's learned.

Similar to outlining, diagramming helps the reader to visualize the relationships between various thoughts and ideas. Concept diagrams, or concept trees, are very useful visual aids for depicting the structure of a textbook.

Unless you have a photographic memory, you will find that recalling a picture of the main points will greatly increase what you remember. Beyond this, such diagrams require that you distill what is essential to the text and how it relates to the main message.

Suppose you read a chapter in your Biology assignment about the parts of a cell. Your diagram might reduce your reading material to look like the following:

Parts of a Cell

Outside of Cell	**Inside of Cell**
cell wall	cytoplasm
cell membrane	vacuoles
nucleus chloroplasts	chlorophyll

More than a listing of main points, diagrams allow you to picture how parts fit together, which enhances your ability to recall the information you've read. This is especially true the more "visual" you are.

Distill it into a synopsis

The second step in the process of summarizing is to write a brief synopsis of what you've learned. When you need to review the material, diagrams will remind you of the significant elements in the text. Your synopsis will remind you of what insight you walked away with—the main idea.

The goal here is to put in your own words what you gleaned from what you read. You will find this process of putting in your own words the author's message an invaluable gauge of whether you have understood the message—and on what level.

Use this method a chapter at a time, and do not proceed to the *next* chapter until you have completed the following exercise:

1. Write definitions of any key terms you feel are essential to understanding the topic.

2. Write questions and answers you feel clarify the topic.

3. Write any questions for which you *don't* have answers—then make sure you find them through re-reading, further research or asking another student or your teacher.

4. Even if you still have unanswered questions, move on to the next section and complete numbers 1 to 3 for that section. (And so on, until your reading assignment is complete.) See if this method doesn't help

you get a better handle on any assignment right from the start.

Critical reading is not easy. It requires a lot more concentration and effort than the quick-reference reading that you can get away with for much of your day-to-day class assignments. And I won't kid you—much of the reading you'll do in the latter years of high school and throughout college will be critical reading.

But if you follow the steps I've outlined in this chapter for each critical reading assignment that you tackle—preparing yourself for the read, doing a preread skim, followed by an analytical reading, concluding with a summarization—you'll discover that critical reading can be a lot smoother, even rewarding, experience!

The method you probably learned

If you were taught any specific reading method in school, it was probably the one developed back in the 1940s that is abbreviated "SQ3R." This stands for **Survey, Question, Read, Recite and Review.** Here's how the process works:

SURVEY   Preread the chapter, concentrating on topic sentences, subheads and review questions, in order to get an overview of what's ahead.

QUESTION   Once you've surveyed the chapter, ask yourself what information is contained in it. Consider turning the subheads into questions as an exercise.

READ   Now read the first section thoroughly, attempting to answer the questions you've posed. Take notes, highlight, underline, map.

RECITE   Now answer the questions *without* looking at your notes or the text. When you're done, go on to the next section. Continue this detailed reading/reciting tandem until you finish the chapter (or the assignment).

REVIEW   Go back over the entire assignment.

Does this sound familiar? I agree. I think this method is completely incorporated into the steps I've outlined in this and previous chapters, so I left it out of the previous edition of this book. Since some teachers have taken me to task for failing to mention it, here it is.

Frankly, I think the detailed method I've proposed—and the helpful advice along the way—covers far more ground.

Chapter Seven

READING THE LITERATURE

"Will you walk a little faster?" said a whiting to a snail,

"There's a porpoise close behind us and he's treading on my tail!"

"If I'd been the whiting," said Alice, whose thoughts were still running on the song, "I'd have said to the porpoise, 'Keep back, please; we don't want you with us!'"

"They were obliged to have him with them," the Mock Turtle said. "No wise fish would go anywhere without a Porpoise."

"Wouldn't it really?" said Alice in a tone of great surprise.

"Of course not," said the Mock Turtle. "Why, if a fish came to me, and told me he was going on a journey, I should say, 'With what porpoise?'"

"Don't you mean 'purpose?'" said Alice.

"I mean what I say," the Mock Turtle replied in an offended tone.

— Lewis Carroll, *Alice in Wonderland*

In this excerpt, you could enjoy the nonsensical picture of a porpoise pushing a snail and whiting to walk faster. You might laugh at the confusion of "porpoise" and "purpose" by the Mock Turtle. Or you could discern the *message*—that you need to have a purpose when you are on a journey...or reading.

In today's world of Nintendo, Ninja Turtles, "gangsta rap", and grunge, literature often takes a back seat. So much so that many of your classmates (not *you*, of course) may not even know that **Alice in Wonderland** is an important piece of literature.

Why should you care about literature? Who needs to read the book when you can see the movie?

While I didn't write this book to give you a lecture on the merits of the classics, please bear with me for a couple of paragraphs.

The greatest involvement device

Unlike anything else, literature *involves* the reader in the story. How? There are no joysticks to manipulate, no "sensur-round" sound to engulf you. Your imagination is your only involvement device, but it far surpasses any high-tech computer gimmicks.

Your imagination makes reading the ultimate adventure. It allows you to immerse yourself in the story—identifying with the protagonist, fighting his battles, experiencing his fears, sharing his victories. You may become so involved, you end up staying up well past your bedtime, turning page after page late into the night!

Your imagination is the vehicle that allows you to explore a million different lives, from floating down the Mississippi River on a raft, to suffering through a star-crossed love affair, to having tea with the March Hare and the Mad Hatter, as our Alice did.

Creative writing may be serious or humorous or sublime...or all three. It is often subtle; meanings are elusive and delicate. Such writing, when done effectively, evokes emotional responses. You get angry. You shed a tear. You chuckle. An author's expression strikes a chord that moves you. You and the author communicate on a level that is far beyond an exchange of facts and information.

Enough said. Assuming that I've converted all you literature skeptics to avid library loiterers (and even if I haven't), I'll offer some advice to help you begin your journey to literary appreciation. It begins with understanding the basic roadmap.

Which reading method? Pleasure or critical

While I certainly encourage you to approach your reading with the enthusiasm and anticipation that would justify the pleasure-reading method (see Chapter 2), the demands of your teacher who assigns the reading will probably require the *critical* reading method.

Reading literature requires most of the skills we've discussed previously.

There are devices and clues to ferret out that will help you follow the story and understand its meaning better.

You will analyze and interpret what the author is saying and evaluate its worth.

But in addition, in literature, you will be able to appreciate the *words* themselves. In textbooks, you often must penetrate a thick jungle of tangled sentences and murky paragraphs to find the information you seek.

Great literature *is* its language. It's the flow and ebb of its words, the cadence of its sentences, as much as it is story and theme.

And as you read more, you'll uncover the diversity of tapestries that different authors weave with their words. You may discover similar themes coursing through the works of authors like Ernest Hemingway or Thomas Hardy, but their use of language is as different as desert and forest. The composition of the words themselves, then, is an element you'll want to examine as you critically read literature.

Fiction: Just another word for storytelling

Most fiction is an attempt to tell a story. There is a *beginning,* in which characters and setting are introduced. There is a *conflict or struggle* (middle) that advances the story to a *climax* (end)—where the conflict is resolved. A final denouement or "winding up" unravels or clarifies the conclusion of the story.

Your literature class will address all of these parts using literary terms that are often more confusing than helpful. The following are brief definitions of some of the more important ones:

Plot: The order or sequence of the story—how it proceeds from opening through climax. Your ability to understand and appreciate literature depends upon how well you follow the plot—the *story.*

Improve Your Reading

Characterization: The personalities or characters central to the story—the heroes, the heroines and the villains. You will want to identify the main characters of the story and their relationship to the struggle or conflict. Pay particular attention as to whether the characters are three dimensional—are they real and believable?

Theme: The controlling message or subject of the story, the moral or idea that the author is using the plot and characters to communicate. Some examples: man's inhumanity to man, man's impotency in his environment, the corrupting influence of power, greed and unrequited love. Just as with nonfiction, you need to discern this theme to really understand what it is the author wants to communicate.

Setting: The time and place in which the story takes place. This is especially important when reading a historical novel or one that takes you to another culture.

Point of View: Who is telling the story? Is it one of the central characters giving you flashbacks or a first-person perspective? Or is it a third-person narrator offering commentary and observations on the characters, the setting and the plot? This is the person who moves the story and gives it an overall tone.

The first step in reading literature is to familiarize yourself with these concepts—and then try to recognize them in each novel or short story you read.

The second is the same as for reading nonfiction—to identify your purpose for reading.

Allow your purpose to define how you will read. If you are reading to enjoy the story and to be entertained, then a pleasure read is the way to go. If you're reading for a class and will need to participate in discussions or know you will be tested on the material, you'll want to do a critical read.

How long should it take?

As a general rule, fiction is not meant to be read over a period of months—or even weeks. You should try to read it as quickly as possible to get a full appreciation of the author's plot, character and theme. You should read fast enough to progress through the plot, get a sense of the characters and their struggles and hear the author's message or theme.

It's helpful to set a goal as to when you want to finish your reading. Frequently, of course, this will already be set for you, if you're reading is a class assignment.

You should, however, set daily goals. Set aside one or two hours to read, or set a goal of reading three chapters a day until you finish. Reading sporadically—10 minutes one day, a half hour the next, then not picking up the book until several days later—means that you'll lose track of the plot and characters—and just as quickly lose interest.

Too often when students do not establish a regular schedule, their reading becomes fragmented, making it very difficult to piece together the whole story. A reasonable goal is to try to read a novel in less than a week, to read a short story in one sitting. The key to achieving this goal is that once you begin, you should read every day until you finish. By doing this, the story and characters will stay fresh in your mind.

If you try to read fiction more rapidly, you will greatly increase your enjoyment of it. It is vitally important that as you try to read faster, you give the story your full attention By doing this you will be surprised by how improved your understanding and appreciation are.

Improve Your Reading

To speed your reading of fiction, try this experiment:

1. Find a novel or short story that interests you and is relatively easy to read. *War and Peace* or *The Brothers Karamazov* shouldn't be candidates.

2. Set aside two or three hours to invest in reading the book. If at all possible, finish it in one sitting. If you can't, then allocate the same amount of time each day until you do.

By trying this experiment, you will discover that fiction is *intended* to be read this way—whenever possible, in one sitting.

It is as if you are sitting at a master storyteller's feet as he spins his tale. You want to know how the story ends and what happens to the hero.

Will the villain get his comeuppance? Will the hero get the girl? Or ride off with his horse?

You appreciate the story far more at the end than anywhere in the middle.

Some other tips that will help in your reading of fiction:

1. Get the plot straight and maintain awareness of its progression.

2. Take breaks to review what has occurred and who is involved.

3. Vary your reading method—from skimming transitional, bridge material to carefully reading description and narration.

4. Ask questions of the story's theme. What is the message?

You're allowed to enjoy it

A final recommendation: Give yourself permission to *enjoy* what you are reading. You will be amazed at the difference this will make. Fiction, unlike any other reading, offers to take you on an adventure. Through your mind, you can journey to far-away lands, pretend you are someone you can never be, feel emotions you may never really live.

All of this happens as you gain an appreciation of literature—as you learn to understand fiction and allow yourself to enjoy a great story.

Chapter Eight

FOCUSING YOUR MIND

Concentration: It's one of the biggest challenges facing any reader.

Why? Unlike other activities, reading requires an *active* mind and a *passive* body. A deadly combination, especially when you've spent the day in classes and haven't had a chance to burn off that excess energy with a tennis game, "hoops" or a quick run around the campus.

Concentration-wise, reading can be more demanding than class lectures, doing homework assignments or taking notes. In class, you at least have vocal variety and the threat of being called on to keep you focused. And writing, while a sedentary activity, still requires some hand-eye coordination to keep your brain working.

Keep your mind on one thing

Concentration begins with the ability to keep your mind directed to one thing—your reading assignment. This is not an innate talent, but a learned discipline. Much like an athlete must learn to be so focused that he is completely uneffected by the screaming crowds, good readers absorb themselves in what they're reading.

How does *your* mind discipline "rate?" Use these questions to find out:

1. When I read, do I often allow random thoughts to steal my focus?

2. Am I easily distracted as I read by noises or other activity so that I keep looking up from my book?

3. Am I watching the clock to see how long I have read, or am I so absorbed that I'm unconcerned about time?

There is no simple, magic formula for conjuring up concentration—especially when you're faced with a critical reading assignment you're not particularly looking forward to. But if you follow the preparatory steps I've discussed in previous chapters—define your purpose, skim for a preread, identify questions you will seek answers for—you should find it a bit easier to stay focused.

Steps to better concentration

Here are some other practical steps I recommend to increase your ability to concentrate:

1. *Get some exercise* before you begin your reading. A game of tennis, an exercise class, a workout at the gym, even a brisk walk, will help burn off *physical*

energy so you'll be able to direct all your *mental* energy to your reading.

I knew a high school student teacher who had to face a stack of essay papers two nights a week. On those nights, she scheduled an aerobics class before she began her three-hour paper-grading session. She knew that if she didn't "feel the burn" before her work, she'd be burning the midnight oil as she struggled to stay focused.

2. *Read in the right place.* No, it's not in front of the TV, nor in your room if your roommate is hosting a pizza party. Reading is a solitary activity. Find a quiet corner, preferably in a place designated for study only—at your desk, in the library. Although tempting, reading on your bed can be dangerous if you're struggling to concentrate. You just may lose the battle and find yourself in the perfect place to doze off.

3. *Eliminate distractions.* Exercising and reading in a quiet, solitary place will help. And if you've properly scheduled your reading time (see *Manage Your Time*), you won't be distracted by other pending assignments. If you're trying to read one assignment while worrying about another, your concentration—and comprehension—will inevitably suffer.

Make sure there's nothing else in sight to vie for your attention. Letters on your desk that you need to respond to? Put them away and schedule some time to write back. Sirens and screams from the TV show in the other room? Turn it off, down or close your door.

4. ***Plan breaks.*** If you have three hours or more of reading ahead of you, the mere thought of it may be so discouraging that you already can't concentrate. Schedule short 10- or 15-minute breaks, after each hour of reading. Get up. Listen to some music. Stretch or walk around. If you must break more frequently, keep your breaks shorter. By breaking up your reading into smaller, more digestible bites, you'll be able to concentrate more effectively.

Wait! Don't start reading yet.

Have you defined your purpose for reading? Yes, once again, you must have a clearly defined purpose or goal. What are you reading for? (I know we have addressed this numerous times, but spaced repetition is a very effective way to make a point.)

The point is that reading without purpose is the greatest means to getting nowhere, which is where you'll find your mind after about a half-hour.

Know why you are reading. If your teacher or professor has given you questions to answer, then you know what you're looking for. If not, ask your *own* questions, using the clues in your book (as discussed in Chapter 2).

An effective preread of the material should help you define your purpose and stimulate some interest in finding out more—which will result in increased concentration.

Motivation: Crucial to concentration

Motivation, as I discussed in ***Manage Your Time***, is key to your success in just about any endeavor—whether it's graduating with honors, maintaining an effective time-management program or improving your reading. You can utilize all the tricks and steps I've mentioned in this chapter. But if you lack the motivation to read, you'll still find it a struggle to concentrate on your assignments.

There are two types of motivation—*intrinsic* and *extrinsic.* What's the difference?

An avid murder mystery fan, you buy stacks of paperbacks at the used bookstore and spend your free time with your nose buried in them. You love the challenge of figuring out "who did it" before you reach the end. In fact, you'd spend all weekend reading mysteries if you didn't have to complete a reading assignment for your political science class. You're not particularly interested in the topic, but your efforts on this assignment could mean you'll secure an "A" for the term. So you're determined to read the material, and "ace" the exam.

Your motivation for reading the mysteries is intrinsic—you do it because you enjoy it. You don't get any awards. You don't get paid for it.

The poli-sci reading, on the other hand, requires external motivation. You're reading it because you want to earn a high grade in class. Your reward is external—beyond the reading itself.

Whether you are intrinsically motivated to read or doing it for some external reward doesn't matter as much as the fact that you are, indeed, motivated by something! If you find it difficult to get excited about reading your economics assignment, remind yourself of how this exercise will help your grade—and get yourself externally motivated.

And if *that* doesn't get you motivated enough to read for three hours, there's nothing wrong with a little bribery. Reward yourself with something more immediate. Promise yourself that if you stay focused on your reading until it's completed, you can watch that video afterward. Or you can buy that new CD. (Be careful, though. If you need *lots* of extrinsic motivation, you could run out of money!)

The value of concentration can be summed up in one state-ment: Concentration is essential to comprehension. Where there is failure to focus, there will be little or no understanding.

Without concentration, you will see only words on a page.

Chapter Nine

RETAINING THE INFORMATION

The ultimate test of your comprehension is what you remember *after* you have finished your reading—what you walk away with. As a student, most of your reading will be for classes in which, sooner or later, you'll be required to regurgitate the information you've read in some format—essay test, term paper, multiple-choice, true-false or fill-in-the-blank final.

So, beyond just being able to *complete* your reading assignments, you want to be sure you *remember* what you read.

One of my most frustrating experiences as a student occurred during a geography test in high school. It wasn't even a hard test. But as I ran down the column of fill-in-the-blank questions, one stopped me cold: "Name three mountains located in the country of Israel today that have biblical or religious significance."

How much time had I spent on that chapter on Middle Eastern geography? Mt. Sinai came to mind quickly. (My high school years preceded Israel's return of the Sinai to Egypt.)

One down, two to go. I squeezed my eyes in concentration as I attempted to conjure up the text in that chapter. It seems that I could vaguely recall a photograph of another of these mountains, but couldn't quite bring forth the name, which appeared to be buried too deeply in my brain. I groaned in frustration and the teacher gave me a reproachful look. I had read that stuff! I should have known those other two mountains! Yet, despite my commitment to my reading assignments, I just couldn't remember their names.

Well, believe me, although my memory wasn't working that day, I'll always remember the frustration I felt during that test. And I'll probably never forget that Mt. Tabor and Masada are two other mountains in Israel. (At least, they were in Israel the last time I checked.)

All of you have probably had similar experiences of forgetting that important fact that made the difference between an A-minus and a B-plus (or a B-minus and a C-plus). It was right there, on the tip of your brain. But you just couldn't quite remember it.

Memory *can* be improved

You probably know people with photographic (or near-photographic) memories. They know all the words to all the songs in *Rolling Stone's* Top Fifty, remind you of things you said to them three years ago and never forget anyone's birthday (or anniversary or "day we met" or "first kiss day," *ad infinitum.)*

While some people seem to be able to retain information naturally, a good memory—like good concentration—*can* be learned. You can control what stays in your mind and what is forgotten. The key to this control is to learn and tap into the essential elements of good memory.

Improve Your Reading

Some people remember with relative ease and have no problem retaining large volumes of information. Others often are aggravated by a faulty memory that seems to lose more than it retains. Several factors contribute to your capability to recall information you take in:

Intelligence, age and experiences all play a role in how well you remember. People are different and not everyone remembers the same way. You need to identify how these affect your memory and learn to maximize your strengths.

Laying a strong foundation is important to good memory. Most learning and memory are additions or attachments to something you have previously learned. If you never grasped basic chemistry, then mastering organic chemistry will be virtually impossible. By developing a broad base of basic knowledge, you will enhance your ability to recall new information.

Motivation is key to improving your memory. A friend of mine, the consummate baseball fan, seems to know every baseball statistic from the beginning of time. He can spout off batting averages and ERAs from any decade for virtually any player—and, of course, spew out his favorite team's entire season schedule...and most of the other teams', too! While I wouldn't call him the most intelligent guy I've ever met, he obviously loves baseball and is highly motivated to memorize as much as possible about his favorite subject.

You probably have a pet interest, too. Whether it's movies, music or sports, you've filled your brain with a mountain of information. Now, if you can learn that much about one subject, you are obviously capable of retaining information about other subjects—even chemistry. You just have to learn how to motivate yourself.

*A **method, system or process*** for retaining information is crucial to increasing your recall. This may include organizing your thinking, good study habits or mnemonic devices—some means that you utilize when you have to remember.

Using what you learn, soon after you learn it, is important to recall. It's fine to memorize a vocabulary list for a quick quiz, but if you wish to retain information "for the long haul," you must reinforce your learning by using this knowledge. For example, you will add a new word to your permanent vocabulary if you make a point to use it, correctly, in a conversation.

The study of foreign languages, for many, proves frustrating when there are no opportunities outside of class to practice speaking the language. That's why many foreign-language students join conversation groups or study abroad—to reinforce their retention of what they've learned by using it.

Why we forget

As you think about these elements in developing good memory, you can use them to address why you *forget*. At the root of poor memory is usually the failure to train yourself in one of these areas:

1. We forget when we fail to make the material meaningful.
2. We forget because we did not learn prerequisite material.

3. We forget when we fail to understand and grasp what is to be remembered.
4. We forget when the desire to remember is absent.
5. We forget when we allow apathy or boredom to dictate how we learn.
6. We forget because we have no set habit for learning.
7. We forget when we are disorganized and inefficient in our use of study time.
8. We forget because we do not use the knowledge we have gained.

All of us are inundated with information every day, bombarded with facts, concepts and opinion. We are capable of absorbing some information simply because the media drench us with it (I've never read Nancy Reagan's notorious unauthorized biography, nor do I intend to. But, how could I not be aware of her reputation for recycling Christmas gifts?).

But, in order to retain most information, we have to make a concerted effort to do so. We must make this same effort with the material we read.

How to remember

There are some basic tools that will help you remember what you read:

Understanding. You will remember only what you understand. When you read something and grasp the message, you have begun the process of retention. The test of this is your ability to state the message in your own words. Can you summarize the main idea? Unless you understand what is being said, you won't even be able to decide whether it is to be remembered or discarded.

Desire. Let me repeat: You remember what you *choose* to remember. If you do not want to retain some piece of information or don't believe you *can,* then you *won't!* To remember the material, you must *want* to remember it , and be convinced that you *will* remember it.

Overlearn. To insure that you retain material, you need to go beyond simply doing the assignment. To really remember what you learn, you should learn material thoroughly, or *over*learn. This involves prereading the text, doing a critical read and having some definite means of review that reinforces what you should have learned.

Systematize. It's more difficult to remember random thoughts or numbers than those organized in some pattern. For example, which phone number is easier to remember: 538-6284, or 678-1234? Once you recognize the pattern in the second number, it takes much less effort to remember than the first. You should develop the ability to discern the structure that exists and recall it when you try to remember. Have a system to help you recall how information is organized and connected.

Association. It's helpful to attach or associate what you are trying to recall to something you already have in your memory. Mentally link new material to existing knowledge so that you are giving this new thought some context in your mind.

If we take these principles and apply them to your reading assignment, we can develop a procedure that will increase what you take with you from your reading.

A procedure to improve recall

Each time you attempt to read something that you must recall, use this six-step process to assure that you will remember:

1. *Evaluate the material and define your purpose* for reading. Identify your interest level, and get a sense of how difficult the material is.

2. *Choose appropriate reading techniques* for the purpose of your reading. If you are reading to grasp the main idea then that is what you will recall.

3. *Identify the important facts.* Remember what you need to. Let your purpose for reading dictate what you remember, and identify associations that connect the details you must recall.

4. *Take notes.* Use your own words to give a synopsis of the main ideas. Use an outline, a diagram or a concept tree to show relationship and pattern. Your notes provide an important backup to your memory. Writing down the key points will further reinforce your ability to remember.

5. *Review.* Quiz yourself on those things you must remember. Develop some system by which you review notes at least three times before you are required to recall. The first review should be shortly after you have read; the second should come a few days later and the final review take place just before you are expected to recall. This process will help you avoid cram sessions.

6. *Implement.* Find opportunities to *use* the knowledge you have gained. Study groups and class discussions are invaluable opportunities to implement what you have learned. Participate in these—they will greatly increase what you recall.

Memorizing and mnemonics

To this point, we have concentrated on the fundamentals of remembering and retention. There are specific methods to help you recall when you must remember a lot of specific facts. The first of these is memorization—the process of trying to recall information word-for-word.

Memorize only when you are required to remember something for a relatively short time—when you have a history quiz on battle dates, a chemistry test on specific formulas or a vocabulary test in French.

When memorization is required, you should do whatever is necessary to impress the exact information on your mind. Repetition is probably the most effective method. Write down the information on a 3 X 5 card and use it as a flashcard. You must quiz yourself frequently to assure that you know the information perfectly.

A second technique for recalling lots of details is *mnemonics.* A mnemonic device is used to help recall large bits of information which may or may not be logically connected. Such mnemonics are invaluable when you must remember facts not arranged in a clear fashion, items that are quite complicated and numerous items that are a part of a series.

An example of a mnemonic device is the use of acronyms that combine the first letters from a series of words. One such acronym is used to recall the colors of the spectrum and the order in which they occur:

Improve Your Reading

R	Red
O	Orange
Y	Yellow
G	Green
B	Blue
I	Indigo
V	Violet

Roy G. Biv (strange name, but memorable!) has probably gotten more elementary school kids through their science tests that can be counted.

You will find that in business or the classroom, mnemonic devices like this allow you to readily recall specific information that you need to retain for longer periods of time. They are used to remember chemical classifications, lines of music (**"E**very **G**ood **B**oy **D**oes **F**ine" is a start) and anatomical lists.

As effective as mnemonic devices are, don't try to create them for everything you have to remember. Why? To generate a device for everything you need to learn would demand more time than any one person has. And you just might have trouble *remembering* all the devices you created to help you *remember!*

Complex mnemonics are not very useful—they can be too difficult to memorize. When you choose to utilize a mnemonic, you should keep it simple so that it facilitates the quick recall you intended.

Many people complain that their mind is a sieve—everything they read slips through; they never remember anything.

I hope you now are convinced that this is a *correctable* problem. You simply must be willing to work at gaining the skills that lead to proficient recall. As you master these skills, you will improve your reading by increasing your rate of retention.

Chapter Ten

LET'S READ UP ON ADD

We both fear and pity kids on illegal drugs. But we also must face and deal with what's happening to the 3 million-plus who are on a *legal* drug—Ritalin, the prescribed drug of choice for kids diagnosed with Attention Deficit Disorder (ADD), hyperactivity or the combination of the two (ADHD).

I could write a book on ADD, which seems to be the "diagnosis of choice" for school kids these days. Luckily, I don't have to. Thom Hartmann has already written an excellent one—*Attention Deficit Disorder: A Different Perception*—from which I have freely and liberally borrowed (with his permission) for this chapter.

I'm going to leave others to debate whether ADD actually exists as a clearly definable illness, whether it's the "catchall" diagnosis of lazy doctors, whether teachers are labeling kids as ADD to avoid taking responsibility for the students' poor learning skills, whether Ritalin is a miracle drug or one that is medicating creative kids into a conforming stupor.

All of these positions *have* been asserted, and, as hundreds of new kids are medicated every day, the debate about ADD is only likely to continue...and heat up.

That is not my concern in this book.

What I want to deal with here is the reality that many kids, however (or whether) they're labeled, have severe problems in dealing with school as it usually exists. And to give them the advice they need—especially regarding reading—to contend with the symptoms that have acquired the label "ADD."

Some definitions, please

Just what is ADD? It's probably easiest to describe as a person's difficulty focusing on a simple thing for any significant period of time. People with ADD are described as easily distracted, impatient, impulsive and often seeking immediate gratitude. They often have poor listening skills and have trouble doing "boring" jobs (like sitting quietly in class or, as adults, balancing a checkbook). "Disorganized" and "messy" are words that also come up a lot.

Hyperactivity, on the other hand, is more clearly defined as restlessness, resulting in excessive activity. Hyperactives are usually described as having "ants in their pants." ADHD, the first category recognized in medicine some 75 years ago, is a combination of hyperactivity and ADD.)

According to the American Psychiatric Association, a person has ADHD if they meet eight or more of the following paraphrased criteria:

1. They can't remain seated if required to do so.
2. They are easily distracted by extraneous stimuli.

3. Focusing on a single task or play activity is difficult.
4. Frequently begin another activity without completing the first.
5. Fidgets or squirms (or feels restless mentally).
6. Can't (or doesn't want to) wait for his turn during group activities
7. Will often interrupt with an answer before a question is completed.
8. Has problems with chore or job follow-through
9. Can't play quietly easily.
10. Impulsively jumps into physically dangerous activities without weighing the consequences.
11. Easily loses things (pencils, tools, papers) necessary to complete school or work projects
12. Interrupts others inappropriately.
13. Talks impulsively or excessively.
14. Doesn't seem to listen when spoken to.

Three caveats to keep in mind: The behaviors must have started before age seven, not represent some other form of classifiable mental illness and occur more frequently than the average person of the same age.

Characteristics of people with ADD

Let's look at the characteristics generally ascribed to people with ADD in more detail:

Easily distracted—Since ADD people are constantly "scoping out" everything around them, focusing on a single item is difficult. Just try having a conversation with an ADD person while a television is on.

Short, but very intense, attention span—Though it can't be defined in terms of minutes or hours, anything an ADD person finds boring immediately loses their attention. Other projects may hold their rapt and extraordinarily intense attention for hours or days.

Disorganization—ADD children and adults are often chronically disorganized—their rooms are messy, their desk a shambles, their files incoherent. While people without ADD can certainly be equally messy and disorganized, they can usually find what they are looking for; ADDers *can't*.

Distortions of time-sense—ADDers have an exaggerated sense of urgency when they're working on something and an exaggerated sense of boredom when they have nothing interesting to do.

Difficulty following directions—A new theory on this aspect holds that ADDers have difficulty processing auditory or verbal information. A significant aspect of this difficulty is the very-common reports of parents of ADD kids who say their kids love to watch TV and hate to read.

Daydream—Or fall into depressions or mood-swings.

Take risks—ADDers seem to make faster decisions than non-ADDers. Which is why Thom Hartmann and Wilson Harrell, former publisher of *Inc.* magazine and author of *For Entrepreneurs Only*, conclude that the vast majority of successful entrepreneurs probably have ADD! They call them "Hunters", as opposed to the more staid "Farmer" types.

Easily frustrated and impatient—ADDers do *not* beat around the bush or suffer fools gladly. They are direct and to-the-point. When things aren't working, "Do something!" is the ADD rallying cry, even if that something is a bad idea.

Why ADD kids have trouble in school

First and foremost, says Thom Hartmann, it's because schools are set up for "Farmers"—sit at a desk, do what you're told, watch and listen to the teacher. This is pure hell for the "Hunters" with ADD. The bigger the class size, the worse it becomes. Kids with ADD, remember, are easily distracted, easily bored, easily turned off, always ready to move on.

What should you look for in a school setting to make it more palatable to an ADD son or daughter? What can you do at home to help your child (or yourself)? Hartmann has some solid answers:

• *Learning needs to be project- and experience-based*, providing more opportunities for creativity and shorter and smaller "bites" of information. Many "gifted" programs offer exactly such opportunities. The problem for many kids with ADD is that they've spent years in non-gifted, Farmer-type classroom settings and may be labeled underachieving behavior problems, effectively shut out of the programs virtually designed for them! Many parents report that children diagnosed as ADD, who failed miserably in public school, thrived in private school. Hartmann attributes this to the smaller classrooms, more individual attention with specific goal-setting, project-based learning and similar methods common in such schools. These factors are just what make ADD kids thrive!

- *Create a weekly performance template* on which *both* teacher and parent chart the child's performance, positive and negative. "Creating such a larger-than-the-child system," claims Hartmann, "will help keep ADD children on task and on time.

- *Encourage special projects for extra credit.* Projects give ADDers the chance to learn in the mode that's most appropriate to them. They will also give such kids the chance to make up for the "boring" homework they sometimes simply can't make themselves do.

- *Stop labeling them "disordered."* Kids react to labels, especially negative ones, even more than adults. Saying "you have a deficit and a disorder" may be more destructive than useful.

- *Think twice about medication,* but don't discard it as an option. Hartmann has a very real concern about the long-term side effects of the drugs normally prescribed for ADDers. He also notes that they may well be more at risk to be substance abusers as adults, so starting them on medication at a young age sends a very mixed message. On the other hand, if an ADD child cannot have his or her special needs met in the classroom, *not* medicating him or her may be a disaster. "The relatively unknown long-term risks of drug therapy," says Hartmann, "may be more than offset by the short-term benefits of improved classroom performance."

Specific suggestions about reading/comprehension

- *Practice, practice, practice* reading and vocabulary. ADDers will tend to have trouble reading, preferring visual stimulation to the "boring" words. Turn off the

TV. Minimize time spent with Nintendo or other such games. ADDers may well be extraordinarily focused on such visual input and stimulating games, but only to the detriment of their schoolwork. Where possible, though, utilize videos, computers, interactive multimedia and other forms of communication more attuned to ADDers to help them learn. There is a tremendous amount of educational software and CD-ROM material that may work better for ADDers than traditional printed books.

However, ADDers *must* obviously learn to read and practice reading. I would suggest finding a professional or a program to deal with your or your child's probable reading problems. Anything and everything you can do to make reading more fun and interesting should be explored.

• *Organize your time around tasks*—ADDers do well with short bursts of high-quality effort and attention. So *every* task—personal, educational, social or professional—should be broken into the smallest possible "bite-size" chunks. Rather than making the assignment, "Read Huckleberry Finn", break it into chapters.

• *Break everything into specific goal units*—ADDers are very goal-oriented; as soon as they reach one, it's on to the next. So establishing *very* short-term goals is essential. Make goals specific, definable and measurable. And stick to only one priority at a time.

• *Create distraction-free zones.* Henry David Thoreau (who evidently suffered from ADD, by the way) was so desperate to escape distraction he moved to isolated Walden Pond. Organize your time and workspace to create your own "Walden Pond", especially when you have to write, take notes, read or study. ADDers need silence, so consider the library. Another tip: Clean your work area thoroughly at the end of each day. This will minimize distractions as you try to write.

- *Train your attention span.* ADDers will probably never be able to train themselves to ignore distractions totally, but a variety of meditation techniques might help them stay focused longer.

- *Utilize short-term rewards.* ADD salespeople don't do well when a sales contest lasts for six months, even if the reward is spectacular, like a 10-day cruise. But stick a $100 bill on the wall and watch them focus! Those with ADD will not be motivated by rewards that are too ephemeral or too far in the future. They live for the here and now and need to be rewarded immediately.

Chapter Eleven

BUILD YOUR OWN LIBRARY

The reading of all good books is like conversation
with the finest men of past centuries.
— Descartes

If you are ever to become an active, avid reader, access to books will do much to cultivate the habit. I suggest you "build" your own library. Your selections can and should reflect your own tastes and interests, but try to make them wide and varied. Include some of the classics, contemporary fiction, poetry and biography.

Save your high school and college texts—you'll be amazed at how some of the material retains its relevance. And try to read a good newspaper every day so as to keep current and informed.

Your local librarian can refer you to any number of lists of the "Great Books," most of which are available in inexpensive paperback editions. Here are three more lists—my own—of: 1) the "great" classical authors; 2) the "great" not-so-classical authors, poets and playwrights; and 3) a selection of my own "great books."

You may want to incorporate these on your buy list, especially if you're planning a summer reading program.

These lists, in somewhat different form, were originally included in *How to Study* but not in the previous edition of this book. As I revisited and revised them extensively for the new edition of *Study*, it seemed right to finally include them in this new edition of *Improve Your Reading* (especially for those of you reading this book but not *Study!*)

I'm sure I have left off someone's favorite author or "important" title from these lists. So be it. They are not meant to be comprehensive, just relatively representative. I doubt anyone would disagree that a person familiar with the majority of authors and works listed would be considered well-read!

Some "great" classical authors

Boccaccio	Confucius	S. Johnson	Flaubert
Emerson	Kant	Spinoza	Rousseau
Aesop	Dante	Homer	Voltaire
Aquinas	Descartes	Horace	Shakespeare
Cervantes	Machiavelli	Nietzsche	Vergil
Chaucer	Goethe	Plato	Ovid
Aristotle	Dewey	Aeschylus	Santayana
J. Caesar	Erasmus	Milton	Swift
Balzac	Hegel	Montaigne	Pindar
Cicero	Aristophanes	Plutarch	Burke

Some other "great" authors

Edward Albee   Isaac Asimov
Sherwood Anderson   W. H. Auden

Samuel Beckett
Brendan Behan
Saul Bellow
William Blake
Bertolt Brecht
Charlotte Bronte
Emily Bronte
Pearl Buck
Anthony Burgess
Lord Byron
Albert Camus
Truman Capote
Lewis Carroll
Joseph Conrad
e e cummings
Daniel Defoe
Charles Dickens
Emily Dickinson
Feodor Dostoevski
Arthur Conan Doyle
Theodore Dreiser
Alexandre Dumas
George Eliot
T. S. Eliot
William Faulkner
Edna Ferber
F. Scott Fitzgerald
E. M. Forster
Robert Frost
John Galsworthy
Jose Ortega y Gasset
Nikolai Gogol
Maxim Gorki

Thomas Hardy
Nathaniel Hawthorne
Joseph Heller
Lillian Hellman
Ernest Hemingway
John Hersey
Hermann Hesse
Robert Heinlein
Victor Hugo
Aldous Huxley
Washington Irving
William James
James Jones
James Joyce
Franz Kafka
M. M. Kaye
John Keats
Rudyard Kipling
Charles Lamb
D. H. Lawrence
Sinclair Lewis
H. W. Longfellow
James Russell Lowell
Thomas Mann
W. Somerset Maugham
Herman Melville
H. L. Mencken
Henry Miller
H. H. Munro (Saki)
Vladimir Nabokov
O. Henry
Eugene O'Neill
George Orwell

Improve Your Reading

Dorothy Parker
Edgar Allan Poe
Ezra Pound
Marcel Proust
Ellery Queen
Ayn Rand
Erich Maria Remarque
Bertrand Russell
J. D. Salinger
George Sand
Carl Sandburg
William Saroyan
Jean Paul Sartre
George Bernard Shaw
Percy Bysshe Shelley
Upton Sinclair
Aleksandr I. Solzhenitsyn
Gertrude Stein
Robert Louis Stevenson
William Styron

Dylan Thomas
James Thurber
J. R. R. Tolkien
Leo Tolstoy
Ivan Turgenev
Mark Twain
John Updike
Robert Penn Warren
Evelyn Waugh
H. G. Wells
Eudora Welty
Walt Whitman
Oscar Wilde
Thornton Wilder
Tennessee Williams
P. G. Wodehouse
Thomas Wolfe
William Wordsworth
William Butler Yeats
Emile Zola

Some "great" works

A Farewell to Arms
A Long Day's Journey Into
   Night
A Portrait of the Artist as a
   Young Man
A Streetcar Named Desire
A Tale of Two Cities
The Adventures of
   Huckleberry Finn

The Adventures of Tom
   Sawyer
The Aeneid
Aesop's Fables
Alice In Wonderland
All Quiet On The Western
   Front
An American Tragedy
Animal Farm
Anna Karenina

Arrowsmith
Atlas Shrugged
As I Lay Dying
Babbitt
The Bell Jar
The Bonfire of the Vanities
Brave New World
The Brothers Karamazov
The Canterbury Tales
Catch-22
The Catcher in the Rye
Confessions of an English
    Opium Eater
The Count of Monte Cristo
Crime and Punishment
David Copperfield
Death Comes for the
    Archbishop
Death of a Salesman
The Deerslayer
Demian
Don Juan
Don Quixote
Ethan Fromme
Far From the Madding Crowd
The Federalist Papers
For Whom the Bell Tolls
The Foundation
The Good Earth
The Grapes of Wrath
The Great Gatsby
Gulliver's Travels
Hamlet

Heart of Darkness
The Hound of the
    Baskervilles
I, Claudius
The Idiot
The Iliad
The Immoralist
The Invisible Man
Jane Eyre
Julius Caesar
Kim
King Lear
Lady Chatterley's Lover
"Leaves of Grass"
The Legend of Sleepy Hollow
Les Miserables
Look Homeward, Angel
Lord Jim
The Lord of the Rings
MacBeth
The Magic Mountain
Main Street
Man and Superman
The Merchant of Venice
The Metamorphosis
Moby Dick
Mother Courage
Native Son
1984
Of Human Bondage
Of Mice and Men
The Old Man and the Sea
Oliver Twist

Improve Your Reading

One Flew Over the Cuckoo's Nest

Othello

Our Town

"Paradise Lost"

The Pickwick Papers

The Picture of Dorian Gray

Portrait of a Lady

Pride and Prejudice

The Prophet

"The Raven"

The Red Badge of Courage

The Remembrance of Things Past

The Return of the Native

"The Road Not Taken"

Robinson Crusoe

Romeo and Juliet

The Scarlet Letter

Siddhartha

Silas Marner

Sister Carrie

The Sound and the Fury

Steppenwolf

The Sun Also Rises

The Tale of Genji

Tender Is the Night

The Thin Red Line

The Time Machine

Tom Jones

The Trial

Ulysses

Vanity Fair

Walden

War and Peace

"The Wasteland"

Winesburg, Ohio

Wuthering Heights

Reading every one of these books will undoubtedly make you a better reader; it will certainly make you more well-read. That is the extra added bonus to establishing such a reading program—an appreciation of certain authors, certain books, certain cultural events and the like is what separates the cultured from the merely educated and the undereducated.

Read on and enjoy!

Chapter Twelve

READING: A LIFELONG ACTIVITY

And further, by these, my son, be admonished:
of making many books there is no end...
— Solomon (*Ecclesiastes* 12:12)

Well, you made it through another book. I hope you found
the motivation—whether intrinsic or extrinsic—to define your
purpose, discern the important details, grasp the main idea and
retain what you read here. I promised not to preach about the
joys of reading. And I haven't...too much.

Your need to read—and comprehend and retain what you
read—will not end when you graduate from school.

Planning on working? From the very first week, when
you're handed the company policy guide, you'll be expected to
seek out the facts—like what happens if you're late more than
twice.

Improve Your Reading

You'll be required to read critically—and know what statements like, "Our dress code requires professional attire at all times," mean.

Business proposals, annual reports, patient charts, corporate profiles, product reports, sales reports, budget proposals, business plans, resumes, complaint letters, inter-office memos—no matter what type of work you do, you won't be able to avoid the avalanche of paper and required reading that accompanies it.

Not only will your job require the ability to read and comprehend, but so will other facets of your life. If you plan to own your home, wait 'til you see the pile of paperwork you'll have to wade through.

Credit card applications? Better read the fine print to make sure you know when your payment must be in...and how much interest you're paying on that brand-new TV.

Insurance policies, appliance warranties, local ordinances, newspapers, membership applications, and tax forms—it seems like any goal you pursue in your life will require you to scale mountains of reading material.

For your own best interests, you must be prepared to read—and understand.

I wish you the greatest possible success in your future reading pursuits, of which there will be many...throughout your life.

Reading

INDEX

Improve Your Reading